Better Homes and Gardens®

indoor
gardens

written by Eleanore Lewis

Better Homes and Gardens®
Des Moines, Iowa

Better Homes and Gardens® Books
An imprint of Meredith® Books

Indoor Gardens
Writer: Eleanore Lewis
Editor and Project Manager: Kate Carter Frederick
Art Director: Lyne Neymeyer
Research Coordinator: Rosemary Kautzky
Project Coordinator: Beth Ann Edwards
Copy Chief: Terri Fredrickson
Managers, Book Production: Pam Kvitne, Marjorie J. Schenkelberg
Contributing Copy Editor: Patrick Davis
Contributing Proofreaders: Victoria Beliveau, Maria Duryee
Indexer: Jana Finnegan
Electronic Production Coordinator: Paula Forest
Editorial and Design Assistants: Kaye Chabot, Mary Lee Gavin,
   Karen Schirm

Meredith® Books
Editor in Chief: James D. Blume
Design Director: Matt Strelecki
Managing Editor: Gregory H. Kayko
Executive Garden Editor: Cathy Wilkinson Barash

Director, Retail Sales and Marketing: Terry Unsworth
Director, Sales, Special Markets: Rita McMullen
Director, Sales, Premiums: Michael A. Peterson
Director, Sales, Retail: Tom Wierzbicki
Director, Book Marketing: Brad Elmitt
Director, Operations: George A. Susral
Director, Production: Douglas M. Johnston

Vice President, General Manager: Jamie L. Martin

Better Homes and Gardens® **Magazine**
Editor in Chief: Jean LemMon
Executive Garden Editor: Mark Kane

Meredith Publishing Group
President, Publishing Group: Stephen M. Lacy
Vice President, Finance and Administration: Max Runciman

Meredith Corporation
Chairman and Chief Executive Officer: William T. Kerr

Chairman of the Executive Committee: E. T. Meredith III

All of us at Better Homes and Gardens® Books are dedicated to providing you with information and ideas to enhance your home and garden. We welcome your comments and suggestions. Write to us at: Better Homes and Gardens Books, Garden Editorial Department, 1716 Locust St., Des Moines, IA 50309-3023.

If you would like to purchase any of our books, check wherever quality books are sold. Visit us online at bhg.com

Cover Photograph: Peter Krumhardt

indoor gardens

introduction

a new approach

Gorgeous foliage, exquisite flowers, fragrant herbs, and tasty vegetables combine to make a variety of gardens. You probably tend a garden outdoors, but now it's time to grace your indoor spaces with an equal share of beauty and bounty. In most areas of the country, people spend much of their time indoors. Why postpone the joys of gardening each year until spring and summer when you possess the means to dabble in plants year-round? No matter where you live, plants bring the pleasures of nature indoors.

Plants suit all kinds of environments, from the bright light of a sunroom to the subdued light and high humidity of a bathroom. Match them to your time and interests: Some plants survive beautifully with little watering and fertilizing, whereas others reward you with exotic flowers in return for conscientious care. Whether you line them up on a windowsill or group them to create a garden scene, plants enhance our quality of life as well as the purity of the air we breathe.

windows full of wonder

above: **Sunrooms, conservatories, greenhouses, and window greenhouses open up the possibilities for growing traditional outdoor plants indoors. They provide the brightest light for growing pots of annuals, such as geraniums, and vegetables, but they also contain shaded corners to accommodate plants that prefer indirect sun, such as moth orchids and ferns.**

temporary color

right: **Holiday plants, from amaryllis and poinsettias to Christmas cactus and Easter lilies, make cheerful accents indoors for months. Learn how to keep them going from year to year, so their beauty outlasts the holidays.**

a breath of fresh air

Choose plants that not only look lovely but assist in purifying the air. Some plants possess the ability to remove pollutants, such as formaldehyde and acetone, from indoor air and help our health with no harm to their own. Such amazing plants include corn plant, dumb cane, ivy, peace lily, rubber plant, spider plant, and umbrella tree.

easygoing combinations

Turn your windowsills, floors, and tables into garden spaces with a few plants, both common and exotic. Start with an array of trees, shrubs, and long-lived flowering plants. Add temporary plants for seasonal color. Take a fragrant herb, such as rosemary, and turn it into a tree-form topiary. Instead of plopping pots of ivy in front of a window, train their strands into living curtains around the frame. Have fun and experiment. Grow a grass garden on the dining room table, pack a pot with spring-flowering bulbs for late-winter blooms, or plant a grove of bamboo.

Your rooms plus our design ideas and gardening information make an unbeatable combination, whether you opt for easy-to-grow plants that brown-thumbers can enjoy without worry or you delve into a special group, such as orchids, begonias, or scented geraniums.

a beneficial plant

left: Although its foliage is narrower than that of most pollution-fighting plants, the spider plant takes the prize for being both charming and air-cleansing. Its graceful, arching, and variegated leaves as well as its delightful trailing plantlets sway with the slightest air movement.

introduction

decorating with plants

Consider the decorating style of your home when you select plants and decide how to display them. Where you place plants depends on the kind of light they require. Look at every part of a room as a potential home for a plant because there are dozens of trees, shrubs, tabletop plants, and trailers with preferences varied enough to match your circumstances.

As you plan, consider potential containers too. Choose pot colors and materials that complement your home's decor, matching or contrasting them with the walls, fabrics, and woods.

so many choices

Be dramatic by covering a wall with plants on individual shelves. Create a wall of greenery to divide a room with hanging and floor plants or

vertical decor

above right: Small rooms, like small yards, accommodate more plants if you grow them vertically. Train vining plants up poles or around window frames. Attach trailing plants to ceiling hooks and let their stems tumble down.

shelf beauties

right: A group of plants makes more impact than individual pots scattered here and there. The shapes and colors of a scented geranium collection stand out when you display the ensemble on a decorative plant stand.

plants on pedestals. Highlight a collection of one family of plants, such as peperomias, cacti, gesneriads (African violets and their relatives), or carnivorous plants, by grouping them in complementary pots. Go exotic with palms, bamboo, or hibiscus. Treat extraordinary plants as works of art and display them as such. Prune a woody shrub to emphasize its sculptural qualities. Train a flowering vine, such as hoya, around a hoop or coax an ivy into a wreath shape. Consider the amazing colors, variegations, and textures that foliage plants offer (no flowers are needed for impact).

spring ahead
left: **If winter lingers in your area, but the local garden center offers all the cheer that spring promises with bright flowers, bring home a few bedding plants and place them in pots on a sunny windowsill.**

introduction

lights up

The only trouble you may face when selecting a plant is finding a location with the light it requires to stay healthy. Throughout this book we use the following descriptions for recommended levels of light exposure. Use them to guide your pursuits.

High light: Direct sun from a south, east, or west window with no obstructions from trees, buildings, or curtains.

Medium light: Indirect sun or bright light from a window facing east, northeast, or west. Plants do well 1 to 2 feet away from the window. If the only available window has a southern exposure, set plants at least 4 feet away from it.

Low light: Sun from north-facing windows, across the room from a southern or southwestern window, a few feet back from an obstructed eastern or western exposure, and in the corners of a room.

To grow sun-loving plants in a low-light situation, use an artificial light source, such as fluorescent or halide bulbs that imitate sunlight.

how to use this book

Gather inspiration from the planting ideas and room settings shown in these pages. All the projects, from training topiaries to making a dish garden, include step-by-step directions and details on materials and skill levels. Use "the basics" section for the skills you need to grow plants indoors successfully. The plant portrait pages contain information on scores of possibilities, whether you consider yourself a novice or an experienced indoor gardener. Finally, use the list of sources to find suppliers of plants and gardening accessories in addition to your local resources.

bright garden room

right: **Plants that require high light appreciate the unobstructed sun in a glass-enclosed garden room. Without it they grow lanky and produce fewer, if any, flowers.**

accessorize

above left: Even the simplest arrangement of plants takes on special charm if you use an unusual container. The pansies and ivy in this galvanized bucket combine plants with contemporary decorating accessories.

victorian look

above right: A stylish conservatory becomes a beautiful garden setting when filled with seasonally blooming bulbs and annuals. At other times, it makes an ideal nursery for young plants as well as cuttings in the process of rooting.

pick a pot

left: A collection of vintage pots provides an artful display, with or without plants. The cheery pastels inspire visions of spring.

the gardens

tabletop gardens

light	time	skill
medium–high	1–2 hours	easy

you will need

- stone basket, 18 inches wide × 6 inches deep
- plastic liner
- perlite
- enriched potting soil
- 12 plants in 5-inch pots
- green moss
- small accessories, such as pinecones, shells, or stones

basket of color

In about the time it takes to make a cut-flower arrangement, create a tabletop garden that brightens a room indoors, no matter what the weather. Combine common houseplants with annuals or tender perennials. Select plants for their durability as well as their beauty. Ivy, for example, thrives on a certain amount of neglect. Moth orchids survive without direct sun and remain in bloom for months. Heliotrope and bacopa continue flowering for months. In late spring or early summer, move the planter outside to a lightly shaded location on a deck or patio. Or transfer plants from the planter to the garden.

regular care

right and below: Water your tabletop basket at least once a week. Fertilize once a month. Set the planter in bright, indirect light.

plants

1. bacopa 'snowflake'
2. dancing flowers
3. moth orchid
4. maidenhair fern
5. snowbush
6. heliotrope
7. ivy

1 line The container should be no larger than one-third of the overall design so it doesn't become the focal point. Line it with plastic (a heavy-duty trash bag is fine). Because the basket does not have drainage holes, put 1 inch of perlite in the bottom.

2 fill Use enriched potting soil to fill the container three-quarters full. Don't use garden soil, which may contain weed seeds or insects. Select plants with coordinating shapes, textures, and colors that survive outdoors as well as indoors.

3 plant Before removing the plants from their nursery pots, preview your design: Set the tallest plant in the middle (on top of the soil) as a focal point; place upright plants around it as fillers; and position trailing, cascading plants near the edge so they hug the rim.

4 finish Unpot plants and place them in the soil; cover root balls with soil to the depth at which they were growing in the nursery pots. Place moss among the plants for a natural look. Finish with personalized touches, such as stones, pinecones, or shells.

light	time	skill
medium	1 hour	moderate

you will need

12-inch-wide wire basket

sphagnum moss

peat moss and potting soil

carnivorous plants

little basket of horrors

Kids will love this garden! Although most carnivorous plants require the protected environment of a terrarium, you may temporarily display these insect-eating beauties in a wire basket.

Line a 12-inch-wide basket with sphagnum moss and fill it with a mix of half peat moss, half potting soil or compost. Unpot and plant all but the Venus flytrap in the mix. Because the Venus flytrap resents being repotted, set the potted plant in the soil mix. Cover the soil's surface with moss and water well. Set the basket in or near a sunny window. Water often, but don't let the plants sit in water. Mist the plants regularly. They all need humid, moist conditions.

insectless life

Most carnivorous plants continue to live even if they cannot attract their favorite diet of insects. The leaves of Venus flytrap, for example, snap open and shut only a few times before they lose that ability. Until the plant produces a new leaf, it exists the way other plants do, via the photosynthesis process, which takes place in the now-open, older leaf. That characteristic makes it a little easier for you to raise the plants in your house.

Carnivorous plants are challenging. Many, such as the pitcher plant, butterwort, and Venus flytrap, are indigenous to the United States, but they tend to be difficult to grow for any length of time out of their native habitat, which is warm and humid. Duplicate that environment as closely as possible.

feeding time

left: Carnivorous plants trap insects, such as ants, gnats, and flies. Each has its own method. Collect a few insects in a plastic bag and open it near the planter.

wolf in sheep's clothing

opposite and below: Butterwort produces lovely purple flowers that give the plant a delicate appearance. However, looks are deceiving: The plant traps insects with the sticky tentacles on its leaves.

plants

1 venus flytrap
2 australian pitcher plant
3 pitcher plant
4 butterwort

tabletop gardens

light	time	skill
medium–high	6 months	moderate

you will need

- rooted cuttings of rosemary
- pruners
- soilless potting mix
- 4- to 6-inch pot
- enriched potting soil
- stake, length as desired
- plant ties or twine

standard fare

Rosemary is one of the best plants for making a standard, or tree-form, topiary. Its woody stem and needlelike leaves develop into a natural-looking tree to grace an end table, mantel, or kitchen windowsill. To keep rosemary healthy, occasionally mist the air around your plants to boost humidity. When soil feels dry, water to a depth of 2 inches.

stately herbs

right: A rosemary standard, such as this, takes about six months to fill out and appear finished.

root Start with a rooted cutting, either **1** one you buy or one you root yourself. Cut a 3- to 4-inch length of stem and strip the bottom leaves from it. Stand the cutting in a soilless potting mix. Keep the medium moist while the stem roots. New growth at the top or resistance when you tug gently on the cutting indicates that the plant has grown sufficient roots for transplanting.

transplant Select a container between **2** 4 and 6 inches wide. A large standard will be top-heavy in a small pot. Fill the pot with enriched potting soil. Make a depression in the soil, insert the cutting, and firm the soil around it. Set the plant in a sunny spot and let it grow for two or three months until it develops side branches and triples in size.

stake Strip off most but not all of the **3** lower leaves. Cut a stake to match the height you want the finished standard to be and push it into the soil next to the plant. Tie the stake loosely but securely to the stem with plant ties. As the plant grows, continue to tie the stem to the stake at intervals. Allow the plant to continue growing for two to three months until it reaches the height you want, then pinch off the main terminal shoot.

snip and pinch Loosen the ties **4** around the stem and stake as the trunk grows in diameter. Strip off any lower leaves as they develop. Snip off stem ends to promote branching and to keep errant stems from developing; use the fragrant leaves in cooking. Turn the plant clockwise weekly to give all sides of the plant equal light and keep it growing lushly in a rounded shape.

indoor sensibility

Containers of blooming standards and foliage plants provide elements of interior design as valuable as lamps, statuary, or paintings. If you like, indulge in a passion for a favorite plant or plant family by assembling a collection of them. Look at the colors, textures, and shapes of the foliage and flowers with a decorator's eye. Think of tiny aloes shown in the dish garden *opposite*, for example. These small succulents grab attention, especially if you group them with a few other plants in a shallow bowl. Add flowering specimens nearby in colors that harmonize and contrast to create a nifty tabletop garden.

fragrant design

right: **Maintain the spherical shape of lavender standards by pruning the branches after the flowers fade. Water lavender when the soil feels dry to the touch.**

colorful display

left: Flowering plants, including kalanchoe, hydrangea, azalea, and lily, add lively color to an end table near a sunny window. A small painted ladder provides an effective plant holder.

boxed set

below left: A wood and glass conservatory makes a nifty home for a collection of houseplants on a tabletop.

themed gem

below: Combine a few colorful rocks with succulents to make a small dish garden.

indoor gardens |

ivy topiaries

light	time	skill
medium–high	weekend	easy

you will need

- potted english ivy with at least five 24-inch stems
- wire globe frame
- sharp knife
- heavy terra–cotta or ceramic container
- potting soil
- clippers or scissors

vining greenery

Long, flexible stems and a variety of leaf shapes, sizes, and colors win ivy its spot as the top plant candidate for training into myriad patterns. Ivies with small leaves work best for topiaries. Some grow very slowly. This is a desirable trait if you want to craft miniature topiaries for either side of a mantel, for example, or for other small designs. Like most plants, ivies that grow rampantly outdoors proceed at a slower pace indoors. Fast growers, however, give you the advantage of quickly hiding any mistakes you make with clippers because they rapidly produce new, camouflaging foliage.

In addition to topiary, attempt some even simpler designs. Train an ivy around a window frame as a living swag: Hang an ivy in the center or to one side of the window; use cup hooks or plant tack (a flexible, reusable tacky substance) to affix the stems to the wood frame as they grow. Plant a small-leaf ivy in the soil at the base of an indoor tree, such as a ficus or palm. Occasionally clip the strands to keep them within the bounds of the container and prune vigorous stems that threaten to climb the trunk of the tree.

easy standards

right: 'Shamrock' ivy thrives when you train and prune it into a tree shape. Combine a small-leaf ivy with a decorative support that the plant won't engulf or hide.

prepare Select an ivy with at least **1**
five stems that are 24 inches long or longer.
Ivies in hanging baskets often have the
longest stems. Topiary frames usually have
either a wire prong at the base (to insert in
soil) or extra wires that make a sturdy base.
Prepare to insert the frame by parting the ivy
stems in the middle, exposing the soil.

assemble Slice down between the **2**
stems through the root ball using a sharp
knife. If necessary, cut the root ball into
quarters, depending on the shape of the
frame's base. Reassemble the divided root
ball around the base of the frame, so the
trunk of the frame is centered. Set the
plant in a heavy container, pressing the
root ball firmly into the pot. If needed,
add potting soil.

twine Select a long stem and twine it **3**
tightly in a spiral up the trunk of the frame,
then wind it through the globe at the top.
Clip off all leaves on the trunk section. Repeat
the procedure with four or five more stems
until you cover all the wires of the globe.
Trim any leaves from the trunk.

   The ivy foliage will reorient itself to face
out toward the light within a few days.

   Leave the extra ivy stems growing from the
root ball in case you need to replace a stem
or two you may have damaged in twining
them up the frame. After about a week, clip
off those stems or prune them back and leave
them as a living groundcover over the soil.

   As the ivy grows, pinch new growth
occasionally and clip off errant stems to keep
the globe shape dense and rounded.

indoor care

Ivies are easy to grow as long as you remember to water the plants and keep the soil evenly moist. Mist the air around ivies to increase humidity. The biggest threat to a healthy ivy comes in the form of red spider mites, which tend to proliferate in the dry air of heated homes.

Ivies prefer cool temperatures, below 70 degrees, and indirect sunlight. Feed plants every few months, year-round, with a balanced fertilizer in granular or water-soluble form.

formal elegance

right: A tall spiral of 'Plume d'Or' ivy shows off the plant's leaves, which resemble the footprints of a bird. Spiral wire forms are readily available in a variety of sizes.

informal fun

left: Aim for a little charm with an ornamental tabletop chair. The empty metal frame of the seat holds a 4-inch pot of English ivy. The chair frame is an integral part of the design, so clip the ivy stems frequently to keep them from covering it completely.

heartfelt design

above: Create an endearing ornament for a coffee table with a heart-shape form you buy or fashion from a wire coat hanger. Secure the latter to a dowel or bamboo stake.

pretty pyramids

left: Cover wire cones with sphagnum moss to make ivy trees. Train ivy strands around the forms. Prune to emphasize the shape.

twin wreaths

above: Nothing could be simpler than a wreath of ivy. Use one of the many wire wreath or circle forms available or make your own. Bend a heavy-duty wire coat hanger into a circular shape and straighten out the hook end to push down into the center of the plant and into the soil. Don't worry about making a perfect circle; the twining ivy strands cover imperfections. Wrap the strands around the wire; hold them in place initially with plant ties, if necessary.

orchids

light	time	skill
medium–high	1 hour	moderate

you will need

pot
pine bark or soil, depending on orchid
pebbles (optional)
dowel or stake

exotic allure

Few plants intrigue gardeners as orchids do. If you think you can't grow them or that you need a greenhouse for them, think again. Many orchids, including the delicate-looking moth orchid and the large-bloom cattleyas (*right*), make excellent houseplants that produce extraordinary blooms.

To thrive in your home, orchids require the same kind of attention you give your other plants, but watering is most important. With some exceptions, keep the potting medium moist but don't let the plants sit in water. This generally entails watering once a week. When growing cattleyas, allow the potting medium (porous ground bark) to dry out between waterings.

Occasionally mist the air around the plants to increase humidity. Or, set pots in a pebble-lined tray filled with water to just below the bottom of the pots. When the plants are in active growth (producing roots, stems, and flowers), feed them weekly with a water-soluble orchid fertilizer. When the plants settle into a resting period and don't grow, fertilize every other week. Follow the repotting directions *opposite* as needed.

prom-night orchid

right: One cattleya, the corsage orchid, makes a bold statement as the blooms reach a width of 4 to 6 inches. Give it center stage in the bright light of an east or lightly shaded south window. Smooth, glossy, and medium-green leaves indicate a healthy plant. Dark green, limp leaves indicate inadequate light. Shriveled or pale leaves suggest a lack of water or food.

1 timing Repot your orchid when the roots become crowded and grow over the edge of the pot or when the medium breaks down, usually every three years. Repot in warm weather when the plant finishes blooming and new roots are forming.

2 preparation Soak the new potting medium (pine bark or soil) in water overnight. If the old medium is dry, water it well because it's easier to remove from the roots when moist. Unpot the plant, remove potting medium, and trim any dead or damaged roots.

3 potting If desired, place a layer of pebbles in the bottom of the pot. Set the orchid in the pot; place those with horizontal stems (rhizomes), such as cattleyas, so the rhizome sits 1 inch below the rim. Fill the pot with the medium.

4 finishing Work the medium around the roots and pack it down firmly until the plant seems stable. Make sure rhizomes (if present) remain at or near the surface. If you need to stake the plant for stability, do it now with a dowel or similar device.

a bit of natural history

In their native tropical habitats, orchids often grow on tree trunks and limbs. As epiphytes, these plants take moisture and nutrients from the air around them, not from soil. Indoors, they grow best in a loose, porous medium, such as pine bark, or a mix formulated for orchids. Such mixes may include bark, sphagnum moss, and charcoal.

beauty under glass

below: Lady's slipper orchids look pretty when displayed under a bell jar, but they need air and several hours of indirect sun each day.

great orchids for beginners

- ascocenda
- cattleya alliance
- dendrobium
- epidendrum
- jewel
- lady's slipper
- masdevallia
- moth orchid
- oncidium
- cattleya

floral design

far left: Moth orchid, lady's slipper, and *laelia* adapt to windowsill culture in an east or shaded south exposure. Don't let their growing medium dry out.

cockleshell blooms

top: When mature, *Epidendrum cochleatum* typically produces its upside-down blooms from summer to fall. It grows well in an east-facing window or near a south-facing one.

petite beauties

center: Sarcochilus 'Melba' (tall pot) likes bright light, whereas *Dendrobium aberrans* prefers indirect light. Feed weekly with a fertilizer diluted to half-strength.

small-scale delight

bottom: Oncidium 'Twinkle Fragrant Fantasy' is a charming miniature that produces sprays of flowers. Grow it in a bright window that receives no midday sun.

holiday plants

light	time	skill
medium	1 hour	easy

you will need

amaryllis bulb

4- or 6-inch pot (only 2 inches wider than bulb)

sterilized, enriched potting soil

perlite or vermiculite

paper/plastic cup

fertilizer

holiday hues

No matter what the time of year, seasonal flowering and foliage plants make great gifts. Amaryllis and poinsettias grow year-round as houseplants except in the very warmest climates. Others, including azaleas and dwarf evergreen trees, take to indoor culture on a temporary basis. They don't fare well in overheated rooms during winter, especially in homes with hot-air heat, where the atmosphere is warm and dry. Alleviate that situation by grouping plants, misting around (not directly on) the foliage, or setting pots on pebble-lined trays filled with water to just below the pot bottoms.

keeping amaryllis

After the flower fades, cut off the stem; leave the foliage on the bulb. Water regularly and fertilize two to three times a month with a water-soluble fertilizer, or use a granular slow-release fertilizer. In mid- to late summer, stop watering so the soil dries out. In early fall, carefully remove the bulb from the pot, cut off dead foliage, and store the bulb in a cool (around 50 degrees), dark place for about eight to 10 weeks. Repot it in a container only slightly larger than the bulb itself. Place the pot in a sunny location and resume watering. When the plant begins to grow, start fertilizing again.

beautiful presence

right: **Few other plants present the awesome radiance of an amaryllis in bloom.**

soak Select large bulbs because they **1** often produce more than one flower stalk. Soak the roots in water for one to two hours. Remove any dead or damaged roots.

prepare Choose a pot only slightly **2** larger than the bulb because amaryllis likes to be crowded. Fill the pot halfway with an enriched potting medium mixed with a handful of perlite or vermiculite. Make a well in the soil with a plastic or paper cup.

plant Set the amaryllis bulb in the well, **3** settling it firmly and being careful to avoid damaging the roots. Keep the bulb centered within the pot to give all the roots room to spread out.

finish Fill the pot with soil, covering **4** the bulb up to its neck. Let the top of the bulb peak out of the soil. Water thoroughly. Set the pot in a sunny location. As the flower stem begins to grow, rotate the pot every few days so the stem grows straight.

amaryllis evolution

below: Take time to watch an amaryllis mature from bulb to stem and bud to full bloom. The two-month process inspires wonder in people of all ages. Most amaryllis flower stems, like this one, are sturdy enough to stand straight and tall on their own, but some require support.

not a flash in the pot

The deep green leaves of poinsettias remain attractive long after their colorful bracts (similar to leaves, not flowers) have faded. Keeping the plants as foliage houseplants involves easy care. Water so the soil is evenly moist and fertilize monthly. When the bracts fade, cut the whole plant back to about 8 inches; continue regular care. In late spring or early summer, put the plant outdoors in shade. Bring it back indoors in mid-September. If you want to have colorful bracts again for the holidays, set the plant in total darkness for 14 hours a day, beginning in early October. Any light during this time interferes with the process, so select an unused closet or place a cardboard box over the plant. Continue the dark treatment for 10 weeks.

evergreen ornaments

Potted conifers, such as dwarf spruces and pines, make excellent indoor plants for winter, whether you set them on a table unadorned or dress them up with a few lightweight decorations. Avoid strings of lights except for a limited time. When spring arrives, transplant them outdoors into larger containers or the ground. Evergreens fare best in cool rooms. To keep them growing happily indoors every winter, put them outdoors in summer.

simple setting

right: Dress up dwarf cypress trees planted in painted buckets with collars of burlap or ribbon.

great gift plants

- amaryllis
- azalea
- blue spruce
- camellia
- cyclamen
- dwarf alberta spruce
- easter lily
- gardenia
- heather
- holiday cactus
- juniper
- norfolk island pine
- poinsettia
- rosemary

cover up

top left: If your gift plant arrives with its pot wrapped in foil or paper, unwrap it so the plant's roots won't rot from waterlogged soil. Camouflage the plastic pot by setting it in a basket with a liner or pot saucer to catch draining water.

newer looks

left: Pick a festive color other than red. Poinsettia bracts also grow in bicolors as well as shades of yellow, pink, and cream.

festive group

above: Make a foursome with false cypress, a dwarf spruce, 'Blue Star' juniper, and European cypress.

holiday plants

bringing outdoors in

In the midst of winter, flowering plants bring a special touch of spring to the indoors. Many of the plants you find for sale or receive as gifts during the holiday season, such as hibiscus and cyclamen, are native to warm regions. They're raised in greenhouses and come into bloom out of season. With minimal gardening skills and occasional misting to alleviate dry air indoors, you'll enjoy their flowers as temporary additions to your household. When warm spring weather arrives, set them outdoors. Transplant hardy plants, including evergreens and some azaleas, into the garden after the soil warms. They'll remain attractive and rebloom.

cyclamen

above: Keep the lovely cyclamen healthy for a longer period by placing it in a cool location and watering regularly. Be careful not to overwater.

spring flowers

right: Azaleas that normally bloom outdoors in spring also survive and bloom quite well indoors for a limited time. Purchase plants in bud or flower. Keep the plants in a cool location in indirect sunlight—set them back from a window facing south.

holiday color

left: Hibiscus produce large, striking flowers indoors or outdoors. They survive in cold regions only if you bring them indoors from early fall through late spring. Decorate them for the holidays with a minimum of fuss by tucking a few evergreen branches and colorful bows in hues into the pots.

tender bulbs

below left: In cold climates, tender bulbs, such as calla lilies, can be grown indoors near a window where they receive bright, direct sunlight. The deep green, swordlike leaves of calla lilies accent the curving shape of the blooms. Water the soil so it is evenly moist but not soggy. In warm regions, grow calla lilies outdoors for summer blooms. The bulbs make great gifts. As a bonus, pot the bulbs in soil before you give them to a gardening friend.

festive shades

left: The foliage of *Cryptanthus*, a tropical bromeliad, sports subtle shades of red, cream, and green. Set the plants in ordinary pots painted silver. Group them on a windowsill or end table, exposing the plants to indirect light.

forcing bulbs

light	time	skill
low–medium	1–2 hours	easy

you will need

- container
- all–purpose potting soil
- mix of bulbs: daffodils, grape hyacinths, striped squill, dwarf irises
- bulb fertilizer
- label

flowers in winter

Get a jump on spring by forcing bulbs into bloom indoors. Forcing means mimicking nature and its seasons, thereby inducing plants to bloom as if it were spring. Most bulbs require 12 weeks of cold treatment (an imitation of outdoor winter conditions) before they begin to bloom.

plants

1 daffodils
2 grape hyacinths
3 striped squill
4 danford irises
5 netted irises

1 fill Fill a clean pot that has drainage holes with enough soil so that the bases of the bulbs sit at least 2 inches above the bottom of the pot and the tops of the bulbs are even with the rim. Mix a handful of bulb fertilizer in with the soil before you begin to plant. Don't pack the soil; bulbs need loose soil with good drainage. Choose a combination of bulbs with similar chilling needs for a bouquet of color but use plants with different chilling needs to stagger the show of flowers.

2 plant Set the bulbs on the soil with their growing tips facing up. Ignore the spacing you would normally use outdoors; place the bulbs close together but not quite touching each other or the edge of the pot. Group bulbs of similar type and size. Layer bulbs of varying sizes, with the largest bulbs on the bottom layer, the smallest bulbs on top, and a sprinkle of soil in between.

3 water Cover the bulbs with more soil. Water the container thoroughly. Label the pot with the bulb names and the planting date. Put the pot in a cold (35 to 50 degrees), dark place, such as a refrigerator, an unheated basement or a garage, or a cold frame. Check the pot occasionally and water if the soil feels dry. Move the pots to a cool room with indirect sunlight when the stems are 1 to 2 inches high, then to a warm, bright spot when shoots grow about 4 inches tall.

indoor gardens | **37**

light	time	skill
low–medium	1–2 hours	easy

you will need

hyacinth bulbs (chilled for 12–14 weeks)

jars and glasses, each with 2-inch–wide opening

twigs (optional)

wire (optional)

watery blooms

Hyacinth bulbs force easily in water. In Victorian times, people forced them in hourglass-shape vases called hyacinth glasses. Nowadays a jar or other common container with a narrow neck works well by supporting the base of the bulb and holding it at the water's surface.

Hyacinths forced in water have used up all the bulbs' energy. Unlike potted bulbs, they will not rebloom if you plant them out in the garden. Enjoy their beauty and fragrance during winter, then discard them when the flowers begin to fade.

Other bulbs that will survive in water include tazetta narcissus paper-whites, mini daffodils, crocuses, 'Jingle Bell' tulips, amaryllis, and grape hyacinths.

For an eye-catching, dramatic effect, grow the bulbs inside a tall, clear, cylindrical vase. Put stones or shells in the bottom third and add water to the base of the bulbs. The flower stems grow within the cylinder; the flowers either bloom inside or extend above the vase.

iridescent color

right: Force hyacinths in glass vases not only for the jewellike colors of the blooms but also for their delightfully sweet fragrance, which fills a room with the scent of spring.

1 prime specimen At a garden center or nursery, select large, firm bulbs for forcing, or purchase them from a mail-order supplier. Choose from a range of colors, including pink, lavender, white, purple, blue, and yellow. Chill the bulbs for 12 to 14 weeks by putting them in a paper bag and placing it at the back of the refrigerator.

2 improvise Sprout hyacinths by placing each bulb or group of bulbs on top of a container filled with water that just touches the flat bottom of the bulb. For widemouthed jars, fashion a framework of twigs by crisscrossing them and securing the intersections with fine wire. Don't immerse the bulbs in water or they'll rot.

Set containers in a place away from light and heat until roots develop and 2-inch green shoots emerge. The process takes about two weeks. Keep the water level high enough to immerse the roots.

Move the containers into a warm, sunlit location. Blooms will begin to appear within three to four weeks.

forcing bulbs

timing is everything

It's possible to schedule the bloom time of bulbs you force indoors, although the timing won't be exact. Flowering depends on when you begin the cooling process and, subsequently, when you bring the bulbs into a warm, sunny location.

Force almost any bulb and plant a variety at staggered times to enjoy various flowers throughout the winter. In addition to daffodils and tulips, plant crocuses, snowdrops, netted irises, and winter aconite. Glory-of-the-snow and snowdrops also thrive but prefer a location that receives indirect sun.

Don't force these bulbs indoors again. Transplant them outdoors in the garden in spring; fertilize them when you plant. They'll bloom again at their natural season within two years.

early spring show

above right: For a preview of spring, fill plastic-lined baskets with at least two dozen white crocuses and blue *Iris reticulata*. If you like, cover the soil with sphagnum moss.

tulipmania

right: Short-stemmed species tulip, such as *Tulipa greggii* and *T. kaufmannia* (with variegated leaves), fill low bowls and baskets for colorful, cheerful centerpieces.

turning heads

left: Tulips turn their heads and stretch toward sunlight. Remember that when you set the blooming bulbs on a table near a window. Just as you turn most potted plants occasionally to give every side an equal opportunity for sun, move tulips as well. The blooms will grow upright and evenly instead of becoming gangly.

sprouting leaves

below: The easiest bulbs to bring into bloom? Paper-white narcissus. In fact, if you don't plant them when you purchase them, they're likely to begin growing as they sit on your kitchen counter. Pot the bulbs in soil or anchor them in a shallow container of gravel. Paper-whites produce delicate blooms and a strong perfume.

indoor gardens | **41**

windowsill gardens

easy beauty

Create a garden where you thought you had no room for one: indoors on a windowsill with eastern or southern exposure.

Start a windowsill garden by taking cuttings from some of your favorite indoor and outdoor plants and rooting them in water. Use pruners or a sharp knife to cut a 3- or 4-inch stem; strip off the bottom leaves and place the cut stem in a small container of water. If you like, choose colorful containers and set them on a windowsill for a pretty effect.

Enjoy the cuttings during the colder winter months, then transplant them into containers and set them outdoors for the summer. Some, such as gardenia, are hardy enough to live outdoors year-round in warm, frost-free areas. Others, such as coleus, begonia, and purple passion plant (shown *at right*), thrive in a shady, protected place outdoors in summer, but you need to bring them indoors before temperatures drop in fall.

Although it doesn't suit every plant, rooting plants in water is the easiest propagation method. Change the water in the containers weekly because stale water turns cloudy and detracts from the attractiveness of the arrangement. More importantly, bacteria may develop and create an unhealthy medium for the plants.

plants

1 angelwing begonia

2 hoya

3 swedish ivy

4 wandering jew

5 purple passion plant

6 coleus

7 coleus

8 gardenia

different strokes

Most plants thrive for only a limited time without soil in which to spread their roots. When you transplant rooted cuttings into a pot of potting mix, remember that the roots they form in water are finer and more fragile than those they develop in soil. For at least a week after transplanting, keep the potting mix moist to avoid shocking the plants and to allow new roots a chance to grow. However, cuttings that are rooted in soil should be watered only when they're placed in a pot of soil to begin developing, and not again until the soil is almost dry.

watery home

left and opposite:
Glass bottles and vases in a rainbow of colors set off a collection of stem cuttings on a sunny windowsill.

indoor gardens | **43**

herbs at hand

Few traditional outdoor plants are as easy to grow indoors as herbs. Raise them from cuttings or seeds. Place the plants in your sunniest window (preferably one facing south or east, where trees and buildings don't obstruct the light). A kitchen windowsill keeps the herbs within easy reach when cooking, and pots of herbs make great centerpieces in the dining room on a temporary basis. Some herbs, such as various mints, tarragon, and thyme, grow well in hanging planters. Mints tend to produce

salad fixings

right: Grow leaf lettuces and herbs in an old tool carrier for an attractive and useful display. Set the seedling garden near a south-facing window. Use fresh or dried herbs, such as tarragon, to flavor blends of vinegar and olive oil for tasty salad dressings.

smaller leaves when you grow them indoors, but they are just as flavorful. Tarragon succeeds best if you make root divisions or take stem cuttings instead of digging up the whole plant from the garden and attempt to move it indoors.

care tips

Because most herbs are fairly drought-resistant, they grow well in pots, but when you combine two or three in the same container, they must be compatible in their moisture requirements.

In heated homes during winter, mist around the plants frequently to circumvent the dry air, which leads to brown leaf tips and spider mites. Rosemary is particularly susceptible to the latter.

Fertilize herbs once a month or incorporate a slow-release plant food in the soil before planting. Herbs produce the best flavor if you do not overfeed them.

Give plants a quarter-turn weekly to expose all sides to the sun.

herbal still life
above left: **Create a study in green and brown with terra-cotta pots and rosemary, thyme, marjoram, and basil. Plant in separate containers to attend individually to each herb's moisture needs.**

window-box garden
left: **Fill a narrow window box with herbs, including basil, oregano, and thyme. They'll always be handy for snipping into salads and soups.**

indoor farming

Starting vegetables from seeds indoors is fun, whether you transplant them into the garden in spring or grow them indoors any time of year. Although the harvest will be smaller than what you'd reap from an outdoor garden, picking fresh lettuce, tomatoes, and peas in the middle of winter brings a special delight.

You need a few sunny windowsills or supplemental lighting to grow vegetables, which require at least six hours of direct sun daily. Plant dwarf or patio varieties of vegetables in pots, window boxes, or improvised containers. Hanging baskets make suitable homes for tomatoes, beans, cucumbers, lettuce, and radishes. Train pole beans up tepees or trellises that you make with bamboo poles, or string monofilament from a windowsill planter to the top of the window frame and guide the stems into a living curtain.

Make decorative arrangements by combining different crops in one container. Plant red- and green-leaf lettuce together, for example, or edge a container holding a patio tomato with leaf lettuce and radishes.

Fertilize vegetables every two weeks. Water to keep the soil evenly moist, especially when they begin to flower and produce fruit. Help fruit production by lightly brushing plants with your hand to spread pollen as they bloom.

Indoor vegetables often have less flavor than those you grow outdoors, but they definitely have more than most of what you buy at the store.

leafy lettuce

above: Grow a cup of lettuce. Because there are no drainage holes in the bottom of such a container, water very carefully so moisture doesn't collect at the bottom and rot the seedlings.

great indoor vegetables

- bush beans
- bush tomato
- carrots
- cherry tomatoes
- cucumbers
- loose-leaf lettuce
- patio tomatoes
- peas
- pole beans
- radishes
- scallions
- spinach

a peck of peas

left: Start pea seeds in decorative egg cups. Transplant them to a large pot.

tomato seedlings

below left: Get a head start on your outdoor garden by sowing tomato seeds in a tin; cover with a cloche to preserve moisture.

pick a radish

below right: Radishes are quick and easy to grow indoors.

indoor gardens | **47**

windowsill gardens

light	time	skill
medium–high	1–2 hours	easy

you will need

cedar window box,
26 inches long ×
6 inches wide ×
6 inches deep

all-purpose
potting soil

soil scoop

houseplants, herbs

green moss or
sphagnum peat moss

glass ornaments

decorative concrete
statuary

create a scene

This decorative planting looks as good on a mantel or side table as it does on a windowsill. Change the accessories to suit a particular holiday or season. Make it easy to change the plantings by leaving plants in their nursery pots, as an alternative to planting them in soil when placing them in the window box. Use clumps of moss to camouflage the pot rims. If desired, move the planter outdoors to continue growing through summer. Set it in light shade and keep it watered.

ornamental doings

right and below: **Accent plantings with accessories as you do in outdoor gardens, and change them with the seasons.**

plants

1 geranium

2 oregano

3 peperomia

4 begonia

5 blue ginger

1 plan Gather all the plants and soil. Fill the window box partway with soil; before you plant, set the potted plants on top, rearranging until you like the design. Consider plant heights, growth habits, and leaf textures as well as the colors of the blooms. Figure in space for ornaments and statuary. If you plan to use a stone bunny or other animal, give it the shade of a "tree" by placing it under a taller plant, such as the blue ginger here.

2 plant Unpot each plant as you proceed. If the roots of a plant are growing around the outside of its soil ball, gently pry some of them outward and pull others away from the bottom of the root ball. If you omit this, the roots will continue to encircle the root ball instead of moving out into the new soil. Set each plant in the soil and fill around its roots with more potting mix so the plant is at the depth it was growing in the nursery pot. Firm the soil around the plants.

3 finish Cover any bare, exposed soil with pieces of sphagnum moss or green moss, tucking them around the stems. Water the planting thoroughly.

Set ornaments, such as glass balls, on top of the moss, nestled among the plants. Use statuary sparingly and in an appropriate size for this small space. One statue should suffice, unless you omit the other ornaments. Place the box in a window with some direct sun; or on a mantel in dim light, temporarily.

indoor gardens | **49**

seasonal gardens

light	time	skill
medium	2 hours	moderate

you will need

- wooden window box or clay pot
- sheet of plastic
- potting soil
- prechilled 'tete a tetè daffodils
- grass seed
- miniature african violets

mini meadow

Set your sights on spring by planting a bit of its color and cheer indoors. Creating this container garden requires much less effort than redesigning an outdoor garden. Think of it as a painting in progress: Start with a neutral wash of color, such as moss, baby's tears, or the grass in the planting *at right*, which forms a carpet of green. Add taller flowering plants in the background and compact or miniature plants in the foreground. Orchids, begonias, crown-of-thorns, and miniature poinsettias produce beautiful results. When plants finish flowering, gently pull them out of the soil and place new bloomers in the empty spaces. Water the groundcover regularly and clip or shear it to a reasonable height and spread.

spring cheer

right and below: **Take pleasure in spring indoors with a combination of outdoor plants (bulbs and grass) and houseplants, such as African violets.**

plants
1 african violet
2 'tête à tête' daffodil
3 grass

1 plant Line the box with plastic and fill with potting soil. Unpot the bulbs you previously chilled in the refrigerator and place in soil so the bulbs are about 1 inch below the surface with the stems poking above. Water lightly. Set the box in indirect light.

If you want to and have the space, chill the bulbs directly in the box. Keep them chilled until the stems are 1 to 3 inches tall (12 to 16 weeks).

2 seed Sprinkle grass seed (any type) liberally over the soil surface, covering the soil. The seed should completely surround the bulbs and also may touch them. Water well. Do not let the soil dry from now on; mist it every day or every other day. The seed should sprout within seven days and will be lush and thick in about two weeks.

Use scissors to trim the grass or leave it untrimmed to grow long so it tumbles gracefully over the sides of the window box.

3 finish When the bulbs begin to bloom or after the grass grows about 2 inches tall, add a row of miniature African violets for color contrast. Unpot the plants and carefully place them on top of the soil, in the grass, and in front of the daffodils. With long grass, the violets look as if they have sprouted right out of the ground. Water the violets as you water the grass. The violets will remain in bloom long after the daffodils have faded.

from spring to fall

Combine flowering and foliage plants in a container, as if they were gorgeous floral arrangements. Choose different plants and color schemes to make seasonal variations, such as these spring, summer, and fall plantings in baskets.

Plant directly in soil, in large baskets or other containers. Or set plants (in their nursery pots) in a basket and

springtime shades

above right: Combine shades of pink, red, and white in a tabletop basket. Greenery, such as fern, dracaena, and small-leaf ivy, set off pink and white anthurium 'Aristocrat,' mauve bacopa, pink and salmon begonias, reddish kalanchoe, and red New Guinea impatiens. Brimming with color, the basket looks like a spring bouquet, but the show lasts into summer and beyond if you remove the spent blooms.

summery highlights

right: Line a basket with plastic and fill it with soil. Place tall plants, such as large-leaf, deep green spicy jatropha and perky yellow gerbera daisy, toward the center (you typically view baskets from all angles). Tuck fern, periwinkle, and anthurium around the central plants. Finish the scene with verbena 'Tapien' and bacopa 'Snowflake.' You want a full, lush arrangement, but give the individual plants some room to grow.

camouflage the pots with green moss or sphagnum moss. Opt for a combination of the two planting methods: Plant some of your selections, such as groundcovers, trailers, foliage, or everblooming plants, in the soil and set others in their pots in depressions in the soil. After you remove plants that have stopped flowering, replace them with potted, blooming plants.

Combine plants with similar moisture requirements, if you plant directly in soil. If you just set potted plants among others planted in the soil, water each as needed.

Have fun with seasonal plantings by tucking appropriate accessories among the plants. Use items from the yard or those gathered on vacation, such as a tiny birdhouse in a fall planting; a few shells or a piece of driftwood in a summer planting; and a graceful branch (in bloom or not) or a small rabbit in a spring basket.

fall forecast

left: Duplicate the colors of fall by filling a basket with red-leaf coleus, yellow calla lilies, and orange gerbera daisies. Complement them with blue brachyschome or dwarf asters. Add greenery with variegated ivy, a young palm, and a dracaena.

year-round houseplants

"Houseplant" is almost a misnomer because so many indoor gardeners these days grow plants that are traditionally part of the outdoor landscape. That includes some of the delightful plants shown here. But for the most part, houseplants grow best in the protected environment of a home.

Placing plants in the correct light exposure is second only to proper watering in caring for houseplants. Plants that prefer low light, such as the peace lily and philodendron, wither in direct sun. They belong near windows facing north or back from those facing east or west, whether or not the light is obstructed by curtains, trees, or buildings. Conversely, sun-loving plants, such as croton, cactus, and crown-of-thorns, grow best in or near windows with eastern or southern exposures. Because sun in a west-facing window shines very brightly, place such plants a few feet away from it. Remember that the amount of sun changes with the seasons.

low-light favorites

above: Many plants thrive in rooms with little if any direct sun. These include the striking, fancy-leaf, rex begonia; ivy, which makes itself at home in almost any kind of light; and dracaena, a popular choice of beginning gardeners for its low demands. In low-light situations, plants grow slowly and need less frequent fertilizing (once a month) and watering.

collectible beauties

right: As succulents, peperomias store water in their leaves. They're also easy-care plants as long as you don't overwater them. Grow them for their puckered, rippled leaves in various shades and combinations of green and cream. Delicate spikes of subtle flowers also appear.

contrast and protection

left: A colorful, sun-loving croton contrasts with the subdued dumb cane and filters the light for the shade-loving, delicate-looking table fern.

beginner's luck

top: Few plants forgive mistakes more readily than spathiphyllum, snake plant, and Swiss-cheese plant. They're attractive as well.

shady ladies

above: Anthuriums prefer bright but indirect light and evenly moist soil. Put them on a table near, not in, a sunny window.

indoor gardens | **55**

grass gardens

you will need

- rectangular wood box or flat
- potting soil
- wheatgrass seed
- plant mister
- votive candles in holders

grassy beauty

A velvety patch of green speaks of spring any time of year, even in a tabletop planter. Use any container you like, such as a terra-cotta pot, a shallow pot saucer, or a seed-starting flat. Vary the accessories to fit different moods or themes. Tuck in colorful ceramic eggs for spring, tiny flowers for summer, or wee pumpkins for fall. Give the patch another look entirely by varying your choice of the groundcover. Plant moss that you dig up from your yard by sculpting the soil into hillocks and laying the moss over the surface. Other choices include low-growing baby's tears, creeping thyme, or succulents, such as living stones or sedum.

putting it together

Start two weeks before you want to display the grass garden. Fill the flat with potting soil to within 1 inch of the rim. Sow wheatgrass seeds thickly over the surface and cover with about a quarter-inch of soil. Thoroughly moisten the soil using a plant mister. Place the flat in a sunny location, such as a south-facing window. Keep the soil moist but not wet by misting it regularly.

When the grass has reached 2 inches tall, tuck in the votive candles or other decorations.

focal point

right: Nestled in soft green grass that invites touching, the subdued glow of votive candles lights the center of a table for a special occasion. Change the accents as you wish.

pots o' green

above: Turn 3-inch terra-cotta pots into individual grass gardens to line a windowsill or mantel or to mark place settings at a holiday dinner. Sow grass seed as explained on page 56 or, for a last-minute decoration, dig up circles of weed-free sod from the yard. For the latter, take at least 2 inches of soil with the clump, ensuring that roots remain attached. Let the grass grow freely or trim it occasionally with scissors to the height you want.

plant collections

collector's delight

A slightly fanatical interest in a plant family offers the potential for a great, eye-catching collection. Adore African violets? Silly for succulents? An array of one genus or one species often outdoes a hodgepodge assortment. It presents opportunities to focus on design, especially the colors and shapes of both plants and pots. You'll also learn more about the plants' cultural needs, assets, and drawbacks.

just deserts

Take succulents and cacti, for example. Show off a planting of them in a broad,

plants

1 mammillaria

2 mammillaria

3 opuntia

4 haworthia

5 sedum

6 mammillaria

7 kalanchoe

8 burro's tail sedum

shallow pot at least 2½ inches deep. To create the landscape, fill the container with an equal mix of sand and enriched potting soil, then dig holes for the plants using a tablespoon or tool of comparable size. Work each plant into place: To handle the cacti safely, wear gloves and wrap a rolled-up sheet of newspaper around the plants to use as tongs when lifting and settling them. Set trailers, such as the burro's tail sedum, near the edge of the pot to spill over the rim. Water the plants gently but thoroughly when you finish planting.

Set the dish garden in a sunny location, such as in or near a window with southern exposure. Though cacti need at least four hours of direct sun each day, many succulents prefer indirect sun because direct sunlight can burn their leaves.

Check the soil moisture weekly using your finger. Water only when the soil has completely dried. Overwatering rots the plants, which store water in their leaves. In winter, water every other week or even less frequently.

a succulent dish

left and opposite: **This collection of cacti and succulents resembles a miniature desert landscape. The addition of a couple of small, colorful rocks gives the scene a more realistic look. Various plant textures as well as shades of green and gray provide interest when the cacti are not in bloom.**

display savvy

Once you have amassed a collection, not just a bunch of plants, display them as you would any group of treasures. If you merely line them up on a windowsill, plop them on a shelf, or set them helter-skelter on the floor, you lose the potential impact and interest their individualities deserve.

To highlight your plant collection, give it stellar treatment. Pot the plants in matching containers that harmonize with the type of plant and

birdbath arena
right: Display a collection of plants, such as African violets, in a birdbath. Place the pots in the bowl, using an overturned pot or saucer to raise the center plant. Camouflage the pots with bits of green moss.

foliage or bloom color. Terra-cotta pots, for example, blend naturally with cacti. Unpainted wicker baskets bring out the colors of plants that you grow strictly for their lacy foliage, such as ferns. Plant directly in the baskets or use them as cachepots.

When you group plants on a windowsill tray, on a shelf, or under an artificial light source, vary the heights of the plants by setting them on upturned pots or small pedestals. Include a few nonplant accessories for added interest, such as ceramic or stone statuary, sized to suit the proportions of the plants.

plant-stand stage

above: Begonias produce a wide range of leaf shapes, textures, and colors, all of which make an enticing collection. Plant jewels such as these in plain pots that do not detract from the fancy leaves and delicate flowers. Group the begonias on a simple plant stand for impact.

southwest convergence

left: A cactus collection looks natural in individual clay pots with pebble mulch. Choose plants with similar qualities or contrast the differences in their bloom colors, sizes, or shapes.

indoor gardens | **61**

exotic & artful

light	time	skill
medium	2–3 hours	moderate

you will need

- large, ornate pot
- drill with masonry bit
- broken crockery
- enriched, packaged potting soil
- shrub or small tree, such as malpighia
- hand pruner
- decorative stones or river rocks

foreign affairs

The exotic look of a plant depends on its size, shape, and growth habit. The scent or origin of the plant sometimes play a part as well. Bamboos, palms, camellias, and gardenias certainly qualify as exotic. Many cacti and succulents, such as those from Australia, Africa, and our own desert Southwest, also make the grade as exotic for their otherworldly appearances.

Indoor gardeners benefit from a vast selection of exotic plants from all over the world that are more widely available than ever before. The plant repertoire continually expands and challenges you to discover the beauties of new varieties. Consider the exciting forms of exotic plants with their remarkable blooms. Choose from a wide array of ginger, bougainvillea, banana, and hibiscus varieties for instant exotica.

However, even traditional houseplants, such as scheffleras, look more exotic after judicious pruning. Set them in unusual containers to heighten the effect. Outdoor containers, such as urns, create provocative results indoors.

work of art

right: **Careful pruning turned this Barbados cherry (*Malpighia glabra*) into a living sculpture. Potted in an ornate Malaysian ceramic container with a fish-scale design, it grows as a focal point in an entry hall that receives bright light from a window facing south.**

prepare If the container you select **1** lacks a hole for drainage, carefully drill one in the bottom of it. Use a drill bit made for drilling ceramics and masonry to avoid cracking or chipping the pot.

add Place a curved (not flat) piece of **2** broken crockery over the drainage hole to keep soil from leaking out but allow water to drain. A flat piece prevents water from draining. Place about 3 or 4 inches of enriched potting soil in the pot.

prune Give the plant an interesting, **3** sculptural outline, much like that of a large bonsai, by pruning off some of the leaf stems and branches. However, before you prune a branch, hold your hand over it to visualize the effect of its absence.

plant Remove the plant from its **4** nursery pot. Gently loosen the surface roots around the root ball to ensure that they grow outward into the fresh soil when you repot. Position the plant in the center of the new container, placing it at about the same level at which it was growing in its nursery pot. Fill in around the root ball with additional soil, firming it slightly.

finish Water the plant thoroughly **5** (until water runs out the bottom of the pot). Spread decorative stones on the soil surface to act as an attractive mulch that helps maintain even soil moisture while adding to the plant's artful effect.

plants as art

Plants with striking foliage or flowers or a captivating overall shape, as well as those that are seldom seen indoors, present a dramatic, exotic appearance without much assistance from you.

By focusing on the aesthetic qualities of your plants, however, you'll turn ordinary houseplants into artistic displays. Feature the frilly fronds of large ferns in contrast with the bold, upright forms of sansevieria. Pair smooth aloes with the textures of scented geraniums and begonias.

Reinforce the drama of floor plants, such as large palms, by setting a spotlight on the floor at the base of the container and aiming the light up through the fronds or branches.

Allow individual plants to make their own artistic statement or cluster them for more impact. Set your plants where they'll be viewed from more than one side for the most enjoyment.

living sculpture

above right: A stately palm creates a dramatic interplay of light and shadow on nearby surfaces. Few other plants remind us of the tropics more than palms.

painter's palette

right: The amazing, colorful variegations on some plants, such as this prayer plant, paint a still life as aesthetically pleasing as a watercolor. Group a pretty plant with other works of art to complete the picture.

plant adventures

If you think exotic-looking plants have strict cultural requirements, think again. Some, such as the delphiniums *at left*, take a detour from their usual show in the garden to provide a temporary display indoors and require little more than the usual attention to watering.

The equally awesome bird of paradise and the lovely blue agapanthus contradict their exotic tropical origins by growing indoors without fuss.

You just need to be adventurous and grow an exotic plant or two.

breathtaking

left: **Statuesque blue delphiniums in tree trunk-shape pots provide extraordinary decor indoors. Equally impressive plants include abutilon, canna, plumeria, and fuchsia standards.**

shaping up

Use the shapes of plants to create artful arrangements in your home, whether they grow naturally in spherical, airy, or tree forms or you train them into spirals, globes, or standards. First consider the quality and amount of light a plant needs. Taking a plant out of its preferred spot for a special occasion is okay as long as you remember to return it afterward.

The placement of plants and your choice of containers play important roles in making attractive accents, too. If you want the plant to be the focal point, use unobtrusive containers, such as terra-cotta. Group plants with sharply contrasting contours in matching pots. To link the plants to other accessories or to the overall style and color scheme of the room, put plants in improvised or found containers. For a contemporary look, set large, stately plants on their own. For a more traditional or country feel, mix foliage and flowering plants with harmonizing colors and subtly varying shapes.

focal point

above: The natural growth habit of the jade tree makes it look as artful as a bonsai. Let it follow its own tendencies and the plant will mature into an impressive specimen. Here, in a niche in an entry hall next to a sunny window, it serves as a piece of sculpture. Inanimate statues couldn't compete.

artful placement

left: Plants become artful in many ways: via their training, containers, and placement. In this sunroom, the large spheres of ivy topiaries stand out among the other furnishings. Upright flowering plants, such as forced daffodils, tulips, or calla lilies, become works of art when you plant them in a unique container, such as an urn.

exotic personified

below left: The large, fragrant flowers of the orchid cactus open one evening and finish blooming by the next morning. Also called night-blooming cereus, this easy-to-grow succulent thrives in a sunny window or in a sunroom, greenhouse, or enclosed porch. Set it outdoors in a protected place over the summer.

expansive presence

below: Trees, including ficus, dracaena, false aralia, and citrus, make excellent specimen plants for living rooms, sunrooms, and well-lit entryways. They complement almost any decorating style. Palms, in particular, suit contemporary as well as Victorian designs.

tropicals

light	time	skill
low–high	½ hour	easy

you will need

Nine cuttings of dracaena, 6–8 inches tall

copper wok or similar shallow container

polished black stones, sea glass, or marbles

dracaena poles

The strong stem cuttings of a dracaena species known as lucky bamboo imitate true bamboo with their exotic, banded form. For this particular design, use any species of dracaena, rooted or unrooted. They make a tropical-looking grove that provides an intriguing centerpiece or room accent. Keep in mind that the design is temporary because dracaenas do not live in water, even though they root in it. Plan to transplant the poles into soil after the stems develop several sets of leaves.

Dracaenas make a perfect plant for people who want an indoor garden but don't have time to devote to a routine of watering and fertilizing. Numerous plants survive neglect, but dracaena thrives on it.

When potted in a 12-inch-diameter or larger container of soil, the dracaena plants need watering only when the soil dries to a depth of about 2 inches. Fertilize every two to three months, but don't worry if you forget. In low light the plants grow more slowly and need less feeding. Dracaenas also adapt to varying amounts of light, from the low light of a northern exposure to the high light of a southern one if set away from the window.

create a grove

right: Dracaenas mimic bamboo with their segmented stems. The stem cuttings gradually develop leaves and a more tropical look. Contrast your choice of container with the polished stones, sea glass, or marbles in it.

1 start Start your grove with rooted or unrooted cuttings. Roots, of course, provide the plants with more immediate stability as they spread out among the stones. On the other hand, the arrangement lasts longer if you start with unrooted cuttings. Once the cuttings have produced many roots and developed three or four sets of leaves, transfer the plants to pots of soil. Dracaenas won't survive in water indefinitely.

2 place Fill the bottom of the wok with a shallow layer of stones, sea glass, or marbles. Set the stems in the wok and hold them firmly as you sprinkle in more stones. Work the roots under and between the stones. Begin to separate and arrange the stems as you add the stones. At this point, however, focus on adding stones and keeping the poles upright. Continue to add stones until the stems feel secure and upright.

3 fill Work stems around in the wok, being careful to slide the stems rather than lift them, until the spacing resembles a natural grove, not a clump.

Pour in water to a depth of 1½ to 2 inches. Maintain that depth for the life of the arrangement.

Carefully move the wok to its final location: an end table, dining table, or shelf, for example.

rain forest spaces

Transport yourself to paradise with multiple plantings of tropical plants, such as bromeliads and hibiscus. Grouping the plants shows them off to best effect and helps maintain humidity.

bromeliad tree

Bromeliads, like many orchids, are epiphytes. They take nourishment and moisture from the air and use their roots to cling to a support, such as a tree. (Spanish moss is a bromeliad,

mixed planting

above: Desert cacti and tropical bromeliads survive in a planting because they're potted individually but share similar light requirements. As they bask in the sun, be careful to avoid overwatering them. Disguise the pots under moss or gravel.

gorgeous blooms

right: Tropical plants produce some of the most spectacular flowers: Witness hibiscus (*shown*) and orchids. When you bring them into your house, remember their indigenous habitats. Many lived in the trees and on the floors of tropical forests, so they received only dappled sun for most of the day. All enjoyed the high humidity of the rainy season. Indoors, such plants prefer an exposure with some sun and regular misting.

Tillandsia usneoides, that drapes from tree limbs and produces fragrant flowers in its native habitat.)

Fashion your own bromeliad tree. Secure a 4- to 5-foot multi-branch tree trunk in a heavy container using plaster of Paris and stones. Unpot each bromeliad and wrap the roots in Spanish moss. Using fine wire or monofilament fishing line, attach the wrapped root ball to a branch. Secure it in a crook where a branch meets the trunk. Some bromeliads have cup-shape, hollow centers that should be filled with water weekly. Mist the plant leaves and Spanish moss every week so the moss doesn't dry out.

a bevy of bromeliads

left: It's no surprise that people get hooked on bromeliads, considering their variety of leaf shapes and colors as well as their striking flowers. These grow in a raised planter that took the place of a window seat: flaming sword (*Vriesia*), grayish-green urn plant (*Aechmea*), *Neoregelia* (leaves blush red before flowering), air plant (*Tillandsia*), and Earth star (*Cryptanthus*).

decorating with plants

green magic

Nothing brings a room to life like plants. Their added color and texture brighten the mood and change the ambience of any interior. Completely transform a room using a garden theme, as the owners of this house did, or use a few accessories to augment the plants. Either way, garden-style decorating inpires a comfortable setting. After all, green goes with everything!

In this room, ferns, ivies, and other plants dress up the mantel, where diffused light from adjacent windows suits them well. Alternatively, choose flowering plants for a comparable light situation and more pizzazz. The painted picket fence above the mantel and the Adirondack chairs heighten the

before and after

above and right: **Plants instantly transform an ordinary room into something special. With the addition of Adirondack chairs, floral slipcovers, accents, and the right plants, a living room becomes a garden room.**

garden feeling. Hang a large mirror above the fireplace to reflect more light; open the shutters to create sun-filled corners.

personal style

Use plants as accents in any room to create a decorative environment that brings you closer to nature. Set a large plant or two (citrus, Norfolk Island pine, or banana) near a dining area to simulate an alfresco scene. Give a sunroom the air of a rain forest with a collection of tropicals.

Select plants that complement your home's architecture. Sleek plants with elegant lines, such as bromeliads or orchids, suit contemporary settings. Frilly ferns and ivies harmonize with older homes.

Coordinate plants with your decorating style, too. Choose cacti and succulents for a desert look. Flowering plants fit a country cottage; colored foliage lends character to any decor.

plant happy

Group plants for a more lavish and effective display. Choose small plants for narrow shelves or other limited areas. Use single substantial specimens for a dramatic accent where space allows. Trees create an outdoor aura beautifully. Just plan for their growth and give them adequate space.

In tight spots use tabletop trees, standards, or other single–container displays. In larger rooms, group one impressive tree, two lush hanging plants, and several shrublike plants, such

room for a view

right: Replace an old, drafty window or a space-wasting wall with a recessed, energy-efficient window that makes an attractive nook for plants. Install a shelf for additional display space that's even more efficient.

as schefflera, and fig. Place them strategically as a room divider or as a more casual accent in a roomy corner.

When coordinating plants with your decorating style, select their containers carefully but remember that they're as changeable as wall colors. Choose containers in materials and finishes that harmonize with your furniture and other accessories. The same plants provide different effects if placed in another room using containers of another style.

green room

above: Turn a room with south-facing windows into a cheerful sunroom that invites you to sit, read, or simply savor the light. Place plants on wall shelves of different lengths. Use galvanized buckets as cachepots for trailing and bushy plants as well as for a few cut flowers. Enclose some plants in a tabletop conservatory. Turn wooden barstools, footstools, or benches into plant stands of varying heights.

simple themes

left: Adopt an Oriental theme with graceful, finely contoured plants, such as ivy and Norfolk Island pine or other comparable green plants. Set the plants in bamboo pots and group them with candles in similar bamboo holders.

decorating with plants

all through the house

Pick a place, any place. Some plant will thrive in it.
There's even more potential where you set up
shelves and grow-lights. Make a garden wherever
you find an empty windowsill, wall, or bit of floor
space. When grouping plants, alternate heights, pair
varieties with different leaf shapes or textures, and
combine specimens with the same light and water
requirements in a single container.

Use plants in ingenious ways. Train vines, such
as ivy, Madeira vine, or philodendron, around
window frames in place of drapes. Suspend

pleasant surprises
above: The illusion of twining plants gives an
ordinary hallway unexpected appeal.

curtain greenery
right: Using wire or fishing line, turn ivy into a
living valance by training the stems from potted
plants on the sill up and over a window frame.

hanging baskets in front of a window as a substitute for curtains. Make a swag of greenery in a bathroom that has a bath or shower by setting humidity-dependent orchids or ferns on a windowtop shelf or suspending them from the ceiling there. If your time is short, keep your plants in a room that you frequent, ensuring that you'll notice them and remember to give them the water and regular attention they need to survive.

If you're allergic to mold, avoid keeping plants in your bedroom, where the moist soil might irritate you. For additional safety, keep potentially harmful or poisonous plants out of the reach of children and pets. Set prickly plants away from traffic areas. Don't set plants on televisions, computers, or other electrical appliances that could be damaged when watering.

bedroom bounty
above: No need for curtains in the guest room with flowering plants on glass shelves and topiaries on the windowsill.

dining out
far left: An azalea standard creates a focal point in a dining nook.

bathing beauty
left: Orchids especially appreciate the humidity that hot showers engender in a bathroom.

garden rooms

Gardening, indoors or out, involves puttering. Make a place for it in a greenhouse or a corner of the kitchen or basement. A room designed for gardening needs a floor that's easy to clean and furnishings that take soil and water in stride.

Seed starting, potting, transplanting, and propagating may be messy tasks, but the work space and storage areas can be attractive. Find new uses for old tables as potting benches; turn watering cans into planters. Use stacks of terra-cotta pots, glass cloches, a basketful of hand tools, and garden statuary as artful accessories.

artful salvage

right: Recycled building materials, such as old bricks, shed doors, and discarded windows, make a nifty greenhouse. In summer, vines climb the lattice exterior and create cool shade.

recycled domain

left: In the same greenhouse shown *opposite,* a wooden slab serves as a potting bench. The wood stands on recycled sections of an iron railing. The brick floor cleans up easily with occasional hosing, which also bolsters the humidity level in the greenhouse.

complementary pairings

below left: A vintage wire plant stand comes to life with pots of African violets, geraniums, and ferns. Birdhouses in subtle colors and unusual shapes accent the display.

planter's kitchen

below right: A kitchen counter takes on many guises: potting table in spring, buffet table in other seasons, or writing desk when needed. Plants set in rectangular copper containers lend a summery air to the spot year-round.

the basics

lighting

let there be light

You know that plants need light to grow and to flower. Some seeds even need light to germinate. The light intensity they prefer, however, varies. Plants that grow best in low light, such as philodendron and spathiphyllum, develop scorched leaf tips in high light. Conversely, a plant that requires high light, such as gardenia or crown-of-thorns, produces few, if any, blooms and lanky, leggy stems in a low-light location.

lighting basics

Remember that pale colors on walls reflect more light than dark colors and, of course, large windows let in more sun than do small ones. Light changes seasonally indoors, as it does outdoors, but the sun is always less intense indoors. In summer most plants grow as well a few feet away from the window as they do directly on a windowsill. In winter, when sunlight is less frequent and less intense, move the same plants closer to the light source,

    You can judge the kind of light your plants receive by doing a fairly simple test. Hold a

varying the light
right: Place potted plants that thrive in direct sun in a pushed-out window or window greenhouse. This alternative to a full-blown greenhouse enables you to garden indoors when you might not otherwise.

12-inch-square piece of white paper where the upper part of the plant is facing the light source. With your other hand held 12 inches away, cast a shadow on the paper. If you see only the slightest shadow with indistinct edges, the light is low; if noticeable but not distinct, medium; if distinct, high.

Plants receive high light from an unobstructed window facing south, east, or west. Plants in or near obstructed windows facing east, northeast, or west receive medium or bright light because the sun is more direct. Those in a north-facing window or in a corner of a room get low light.

shading the sun

left: Vary the intensity of light in a room by obstructing it somewhat—with blinds or curtains, for example. Set plants that prefer indirect sun off to the side or back 3 or more feet from south- and west-facing windows.

imitating daylight

above left: Supplemental lights, such as full-spectrum fluorescent tubes, metal halide bulbs, and high-pressure sodium bulbs, make gardening possible in low-light situations—even a basement. Position lights 6 to 8 inches above the tops of plants. Raise the lights as the plants grow.

timing sunlight

above right: Keep grow-lights on for 16 hours a day. Set up a timer to turn them on and off—plants need a period of darkness as well as light. Many flowering plants and most vegetables require more than 16 hours of light indoors to set buds and ripen fruits.

indoor gardens | **83**

a plant stand

light	time	skill
any	weekend	experienced

you will need

one 4×8 sheet signboard, ¾" MDO plywood, cut into: two 65½"×15½" (A); two 34½"×12" (B); one 48"×20" (C) pieces

2x2s: eight 13½" long (D); two 12" long (G)

1x2s: six 36" long (E); four 12" long (F)

four 4" casters with brakes

eight 36"×1½" galvanized metal brackets

deck screws: thirty-six 2"; eight 1¼"

pan head sheet metal screws: sixteen each #12 1¼"and #12 ¾"

sixteen ³⁄₁₆" flat washers

twenty 6-penny finishing nails

two ¼"-thick glass shelves: 35¾"×13½"

twelve silicone discs

two 6' pieces of ³⁄₃₂" wire cable

drill; circular saw; screwdriver; carpenter's square

two ³⁄₁₆"×5⅝" turnbuckles

white glue

classy plant shelf

Instead of trying to find a place to put plants, build one. Outfit the unit with fluorescent lights by screwing fixtures to the undersides of the wooden shelves, guiding the electrical cords down the back.

If you paint the unit to match your decor, fill the screw holes with wood filler first; then sand.

curved sides and front

right: To create curves, tie nonstretch string to a pencil. Tack string 75 inches from center of base; pull string taut; hold pencil perpendicular; and mark curve. For sides, tack string to front edge 21 inches from top. Cut with a jigsaw.

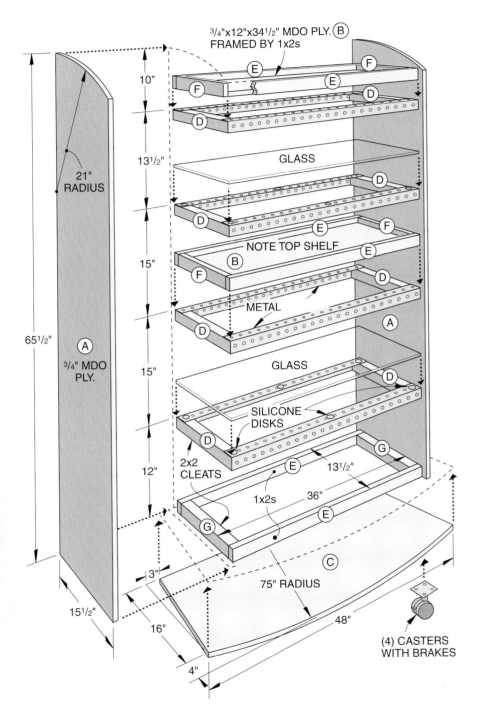

³/₄"x12"x34¹/₂" MDO PLY. (B)
FRAMED BY 1x2s

10"

21"
RADIUS

13¹/₂"

GLASS

15"

NOTE TOP SHELF

METAL

65¹/₂"

(A)

³/₄" MDO PLY.

15"

GLASS

SILICONE DISKS

12"

2x2 CLEATS

13¹/₂"

1x2s   36"

3"

75" RADIUS

15¹/₂"

16"

48"

4"

(4) CASTERS WITH BRAKES

here's how

Precut all parts with a circular saw; for curved sides and front, see caption *opposite*.

1. Lay sides (A) side by side with ends flush; measure and mark placement of shelves and cleats that support the shelves.

2. Glue cleats (D, G) to sides; then drill holes in the sides for three 2-inch screws per cleat. Make sure cleats are aligned before tightening.

3. Attach metal shelf supports to cleats at front and rear using #12 1¹/₄-inch pan-head sheet-metal screws and ³/₁₆-inch flat washers.

4. Center sides (A) on base (C); glue and screw with six 2-inch screws.

5. Wrap each wood shelf (B) with 1×2s (E, F) using white glue and 6-penny finishing nails. Attach shelves to cleats from the inside with two 1¹/₄-inch deck screws per side.

6. String cable across the back of the plant shelves. Loop ends of cables around the sheet metal screws on the top shelf and second shelf from the bottom. Extend turnbuckles to their limit, attach cables, and slowly tighten both turnbuckles simultaneously. Use a carpenter's square to keep sides parallel.

7. Lay unit on its back and install casters with #12 ³/₄-inch pan screws.

8. Install glass shelves, using three silicone disks on each metal bracket to keep glass from touching it.

extra security

below: **For stability, string cable across the back of the plant stand. Don't put heavy pots on the top three shelves.**

indoor gardens | **85**

soil

1 healthy soil Using soil from the garden has drawbacks because it often contains weed seeds, pests, or diseases and has a heavier texture than most potted plants prefer. If you take soil from outdoors, pasteurize it first to kill fungi. Place a 2-inch layer in an old or disposable, rectangular baking tin. Moisten the soil lightly and cover with aluminum foil. Bake the soil at 275° for 40 to 60 minutes (until it reaches 160°–170° on an instant meat thermometer).

Be forewarned, however, baking soil conjures a strong smell. If you prefer, sterilize soil outdoors on a barbecue grill equipped with a hood.

2 mixes at hand Keep packaged potting mixes, as well as the components for making your own, handy in a covered bin or labeled plastic box.

3 perfect potting mixes Packaged all-purpose potting soils usually contain topsoil, sand, and peat moss. Amend them by adding perlite to enhance drainage, and compost, such as worm compost or castings, for fertility. Add water-absorbing polymer crystals to help the mix retain moisture. For growing cacti and succulents, add one part grit or coarse sand to two parts mix. To grow trees and most shrubs, mix in shredded or ground bark chips.

The ideal soil allows root growth and drainage; it retains moisture without getting soggy. The term "potting soil" is generic in the marketplace. Read package labels and look for words such as "sterilized" and "enriched" (meaning the soil includes fertilizer or soil amendments).

time for a new pot Plants growing in pots need fresh soil or planting medium every couple of years to maintain healthy growth. The easiest time to provide new soil is when you repot a plant that has outgrown the size of its pot or has become root-bound. With few exceptions, such as hoya, most plants grow poorly when root-bound. Tip the plant out of its pot; if roots encircle the planting medium, it's time to repot. Before repotting, work some of the roots away from the soil ball (otherwise the roots will continue to grow around the soil ball instead of venturing out into fresh soil).

repotting: part one Move a plant into a pot only one or two sizes larger than the pot it occupies. Unless you plan to divide the plant into smaller sections at this stage, water the plant the day before you repot. Moist soil clings to the roots better than dry soil, and you want to keep the root ball as intact as possible. Cut off dead or damaged roots.

repotting: part two Put 3 inches of fresh potting soil in the bottom of the container. Set the plant on top and spread out some of the roots. Check that the crown of the plant (where stem joins roots) sits at the same level at which it grew in the old container. If it doesn't, add more soil. Fill the pot with soil to within an inch of the rim, working it among the roots with your fingers. Space between the soil surface and the rim makes watering easier.

a potting place

gardening convenience

Organize your gardening chores by gathering all the accoutrements in one area. A potting shed is ideal, but a section of a room, such as a mudroom, or a corner of the kitchen, basement, or garage, suffices. Kitchens and basements offer the necessary running water. Water is one of the priorities for easy cleanup of messy tasks, such as working with soil, fertilizer, and pots, as well as for tending to newly sown seeds, transplants, and repotted plants.

Locate your potting place near a sunny window. Not only will your plants and seedlings benefit from the light, but you'll enjoy it, too.

Whether you design a potting place from scratch or adapt an existing area, build in conveniences. Allow several feet of work surface for your activities. Use galvanized metal countertops for easy cleanup and make them high enough to let you work comfortably. Equip the sink with an arched faucet to facilitate watering. Hang wooden shelves and, if you want, wire

supply storage

right: **Make a place for soil by adapting an existing storage unit, such as a bread drawer, or by removing an under-counter cabinet and installing a tip-out bin. Reinforce shelves, including existing ones you plan to use for gardening, so they are sturdy enough to hold heavy pots and bags of fertilizer.**

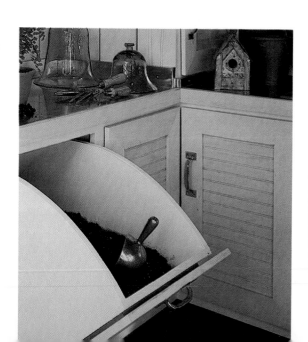

baskets for open storage. Adapt traditional kitchen cabinets and storage units to a gardening purpose. An old-fashioned bread drawer, for example, easily holds soil or fertilizer instead of bread. Utensil trays of various sizes accommodate hand tools as well as plant ties, small bamboo stakes, and seed packets. Use plastic boxes, such as those made for sweaters or shoes, to hold individual components for potting mixes and fertilizers.

If your potting place serves another primary function, keep it clean and neat by hiding the messes behind closed cabinet doors. Make it pleasing with garden-theme accessories.

dual purpose

left: **Display attractive pots, baskets, and tools on open shelves for decorative but functional storage.**

containers

1 **camouflage** Transform plants potted in ordinary clay or plastic pots into pretty portable gardens by placing two or three of them in a basket. Camouflage the pots with Spanish moss. If you want to display the garden this way permanently, protect the basket and the surface under it by putting a plastic liner in the bottom. Water the plants as usual.

2 **pots galore** An array of different containers tempts today's indoor gardeners. Look for planters made of terra-cotta, wood, ceramic, and fiberglass as well as composite and lightweight materials. Opt for self-watering containers if your schedule leaves little time for that important task. A self-watering pot holds water in reservoirs in its bottom; wicking transfers moisture to the plants as the soil dries. Soil in terra-cotta containers dries out faster than in other materials because terra-cotta is porous. Consider this if you grow plants that require evenly moist soil.

3 **instantly mature** Pots develop a patina with age that heightens their attractiveness. Give new pots instant age by sponge-painting them in a random design. Let nature do the decorating. Coat a pot with buttermilk or yogurt; place it outdoors over the summer to allow moss to grow on it. A white crust of salt residue from fertilizer or water looks unattractive. Periodically, scrub it off, especially when you repot, with a stiff brush and soapy water.

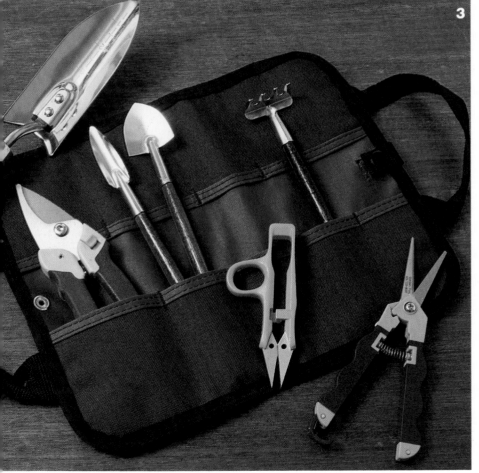

improvisations Make do with nontraditional tools and aids to perform some tasks. Need to pin a spider plant offset (lateral shoot) in place while it roots, for example? Use an ordinary bobby pin. Find other handy substitutes in kitchen drawers and cabinets. Use forks and spoons to dig lightly in the soil. Use a pencil to poke holes in soil for stem cuttings. Place clear plastic cups to make mini greenhouses over small pots of stem or leaf cuttings; it will help soil retain moisture as the cuttings root.

a cut above A knife makes a great tool. Use it to pry plants out of pots, to divide plants by slicing the root ball, and to cut off dead leaves. Take stem cuttings using a sharp paring knife. Scissors are useful, too, for trimming leaves.

prepared gardener Tools designed especially for working with indoor plants make tasks easier and less messy. In imitation of full-size tools for outdoor gardening, tiny trowels, cultivators, and floral snips fit neatly into and around pots and plants. Make short shrift of errant branches on indoor trees, shrubs, and vines with a hand pruner. Use a slender hand trowel to top-dress plants: Dig out the top 2 inches of soil and replace with fresh soil. This is an especially appealing alternative to repotting large, unwieldy plants.

multiplying plants

1 **air layering: part one** A plant that gets leggy or tall without many lower leaves, such as this dieffenbachia, calls for air layering. Via this technique, roots develop in two to three months, depending on the plant.

Cut a slit partway into the stem about 9 to 12 inches from the plant's top. Insert a small piece of wood to prop the slit open. If desired, dust the cut surface with a rooting hormone powder.

Plants to air-layer: dieffenbachia, dracaena, Chinese evergreen, elephant's ear, ficus, and some philodendrons.

2 **air layering: part two** Moisten sphagnum moss in water and wrap it around the cut stem. Enclose the moss in plastic; secure in place with twist ties or tape. When you see roots winding through the moss, cut the stem just below the plastic wrap. Unwrap and plant the newly rooted stem in a good packaged potting mix. The old plant sometimes puts out new foliage on the remaining bare stem. If it doesn't, discard.

3 **rooting in water** Cut stems 3 to 4 inches long and strip off any leaves that would be under water. Fill a glass with tap or bottled water and place stems in the glass. As the stems root, change the water frequently to keep it clear. Transplant rooted cuttings into a soilless medium; keep medium very moist for the first week or two.

Plants to root in water: basil, begonia, coleus, croton, geranium, hoya, philodendron, pothos, purple passion plant, rosemary, Swedish ivy, and wandering Jew, as well as single-leaf stems of African violet.

1

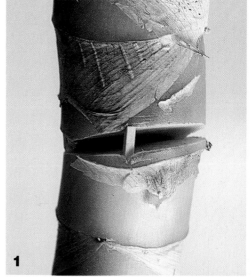

2

3

division Depending on the plant, use your fingers or something stronger, such as two forks or trowels, or a sharp knife, to divide plants that increase by producing offsets. Unpot the plant on newspapers. Gently work through the soil and roots to expose the base or crown. Pull or cut apart the plants, making sure you get some roots with each division. Repot each new plant and the original central plant.

    Plants to divide: begonia, bromeliad, clivia, some sedums, spathiphyllum (*shown*), sympodial (rhizomic) orchids, thyme, fern, and Chinese evergreen.

leaf cuttings Propagate leaf cuttings in one of two ways. Slice the leaf into sections, dust the cut ends nearest the base with a rooting hormone powder, and insert them in a soilless medium or germinating mix. Keep the medium moist while the cuttings root.

    Alternatively, slash a leaf in three or four places. Set the leaf on a soilless medium; secure it with U-shape pins to keep it in contact with the medium. Water well; keep the medium moist. Plantlets develop at the slashes. Pot when they have enough roots.

    Plants for leaf cuttings: African violet, begonia, gloxinia, kalanchoe, peperomia, sedum, snake plant (*shown*), and streptocarpus.

stem cuttings Take 3- to 4-inch cuttings of stems. Strip off lower leaves and stick stems in moistened, soilless medium. Cover with a plastic bag to conserve moisture.

    Plants for stem cuttings: All of those listed under Step 3, plus holiday cactus, gardenia, jade plant, ivy, mint, and oregano.

watering & feeding

1 **watering methods** Overwatering harms plants more than underwatering. As a general rule, delay watering until the soil dries to a depth of 1 to 2 inches. Water at the edge of the pot to avoid getting the foliage wet. Water thoroughly until the excess runs out the bottom drainage holes; empty the saucer. If your water is hard (contains alkaline chemicals), replace soil annually.

Some plants, such as African violets, respond best if you water from below: Set the pots in a sink filled with 1 or 2 inches of water; leave them until you see bubbles of moisture on the soil surface.

With a large collection of plants, reduce watering time by incorporating water-absorbing polymers in the soil, using a hose with a wand attachment, or investing in a container drip irrigation system.

2 **feeding** All plants need a balanced diet of nitrogen, phosphorus, and potassium. Packaged fertilizer labels indicate the percentage of nutrients with numbers such as 5-10-5, for example. Feed plants every two weeks when watering. Dilute liquid and water-soluble fertilizers by half the amount recommended on the label. When growth and flower production slow down in winter, plants require less, if any, fertilizer. Incorporate controlled-release granules in the planting medium before potting; insert timed-release spikes afterward.

3 **misting** To increase the humidity around your plants, especially in heated homes during winter, mist them about once a week. Don't mist succulents, cacti, or plants with fuzzy or velvety leaves.

smelly but good Fish emulsion
makes one of the best plant foods, but it smells bad. Made from fish byproducts, fish emulsion usually contains 5 percent nitrogen, 1 percent phosphorus, and a trace of potassium, for a 5-1-1 solution. It has a slightly acidic pH. Soluble kelp is often added in commercial products for the benefit of additional potassium, which aids root development. Dilute fish emulsion to 1½ teaspoons per gallon of water to feed seedlings and newly rooted cuttings. Use 1 tablespoon to 1 gallon of water for established plants. Either spray or mist the fertilizer on the plants' foliage or pour it on the planting medium. The fertilizer releases its nutrients slowly and does not burn plants' roots or foliage, as some other plant foods do. The distinctive odor usually lasts less than a day; some products are deodorized.

humidity To keep the humidity
around your plants at a consistently high level, fill trays or pot saucers with a layer of pebbles. Set the plants on top and pour water into the trays or saucers to just below the bottom of the pots. Replenish the water as necessary.

The moisture plants lose through their leaf pores evaporates into the air. Take advantage of that natural occurrence by grouping your plants fairly close together so neighboring plants get the benefit of the slight rise in atmospheric humidity.

tips

1   **just a trim** Even with the best of care, plants occasionally develop brown, yellow, or ragged edges on their foliage. Before you get out the scissors, check that the change is cosmetic and not the result of overwatering, underwatering, or, in the case of ragged leaves, a playful pet. Grab the scissors and trim off the offending edges, following the natural outline of the leaf as closely as possible.

2   **proper pinches** Another way to groom your plants and keep them looking good involves removing dying or spent flowers and leaves. As flowers fade, pinch them off using your thumb and index finger. Use the same technique on soft, pliable leaf stalks. Trimming woody, thick leaf stalks requires pruning shears or a pair of scissors to avoid damaging the main stem.

Pinch stem ends on young plants occasionally to encourage new growth and keep them looking lush and full. Do the same on an older plant to maintain a compact form.

3   **one good turn** Ensure that all sides of a plant receive an equal share of light. At least one side of a plant growing in or near a window is shaded from the available sun. That causes it to bend toward the light and grow spindly on the shaded side. Prevent the distortion by giving each plant a quarter-turn every week. Turn it clockwise or counterclockwise but always in the same direction once you start. All plants need this, including larger floor specimens; move those more easily by putting the pots on casters.

selective cuts Remove leaves or **4**
stems that look diseased or dying as soon as
you notice them. Don't wait for them to die
completely. Inspect plants frequently. Lush,
leafy ferns often hide yellowed parts in their
midst. Carefully part the fronds until you see
the plant's base. With scissors or a hand
pruner, cut the leaf stalk close to the crown
or main stem.

floor care Protect the beauty of **5**
your floors and furniture from the effects
of moisture. Water causes damage directly
by leaking from containers with drainage
holes and indirectly from sweating in
pots without drainage. Place pots in clear
plastic or decorative saucers. Adhere
self-stick pot protectors to the bottom of
planters without drainage holes. Raise
containers above the floor or table surface
on plant stands.

over the top Large plants make a **6**
statement in a room, but some end up being
too vigorous for their own good and for the
space you assign them. Some outdoor shrubs
and trees outgrow their welcome by the
front door or window, and those indoors
can do the same. Pruning helps. Severe
cutting back lets you start over with some
plants, such as dracaena and bamboo, but
most plants resent it. To avoid a plant hitting
the ceiling, as ficus and citrus often do, begin
selective pruning while the plant is young.
Cut large branches back to small side
branches to encourage new growth from
within, not above.

7 **going away: part one** Before you leave for a vacation, ensure that your plants survive your absence. Water all of them thoroughly. If you grow vegetables indoors, harvest any that are ripe or almost mature. Protect plants for longer periods by enclosing them in plastic bags, but keep the bag off the plant by sticking three or four stakes into the soil. Move plants away from south- and west-facing windows before you go so the sun doesn't bake them.

8 **going away: part two** Group plants to conserve humidity and moisture. Line a tray with pebbles and fill it with water to just below the top of the pebbles. Set the plants on the tray. Place the tray back from windows with direct exposure to the sun. This method also works on a day-to-day basis for plants that prefer high humidity, such as orchids and gardenias.

9 **summer vacation** Most houseplants enjoy a respite outdoors as much as you do. Move plants outside gradually after the air has warmed up in late spring (when night temperatures consistently remain in the 60s). Set the plants in a location sheltered from wind and direct sun to prevent the foliage from burning. Orchids, for example, thrive in the shade of a deciduous tree if you hang them from branches where they receive dappled sun.

Water on the same schedule you use indoors, but keep an eye on the soil because the heat of summer dries it faster. Fertilize every week or two.

bath time Cleanliness is essential to a plant's health and appearance. Dull leaves detract from a plant's attractiveness. Dust buildup on foliage clogs pores and interferes with photosynthesis. Make it a regular part of your routine to clean plants in the kitchen sink using the spray nozzle; use the bathroom shower for large, bushy plants. Wipe large leaves using a damp cloth. Dust fuzzy-leaf plants, such as African violets and many succulents, by bending a pipe cleaner into an oval shape and brushing it over the leaves; avoid using water on those plants.

10

support, please Some plants need training to look their best. Make or buy small trellises, tepees, and tuteurs to support vining as well as trailing plants. Wrap sphagnum moss around a piece of lumber or split log to provide an upright to which plants, such as pothos can cling. Loosely tie sprays of orchids, such as moth orchid and cymbidium, to bamboo canes to prevent them from flopping over.

11

post-summer care Bring your houseplants indoors at summer's end, before night temperatures turn cool and you turn on the heat indoors. Because plants tend to grow more voraciously outdoors, repot those that have outgrown their containers; set them in pots one size up from their current homes. Check all plants and soil for hitchhiking insects; hose off plants and flush soil with water.

12

pests & diseases

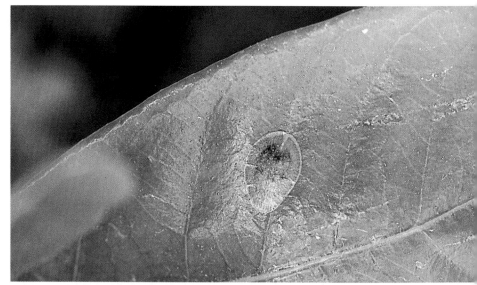

sensible precautions

The best defense against plant pests and diseases indoors is prevention. Begin practicing prevention at the garden center. Examine any plant you want to buy, checking carefully for signs of insects and diseases. In the case of whiteflies, inspection is easy: Brush against an infested plant and the insects rise in a dusty cloud of white. Other pests, such as scale insects and aphids, sometimes require a more diligent search. That includes inspecting the undersides of leaves for insects and egg casings.

Though more harmful and more difficult to control than insects, diseases typically develop in the greenhouse or at home as a result of poor care. Before you buy a plant, look for the telltale signs of problems, especially of viruses, which kill the plant they attack and spread easily to other plants.

Prevention extends to bringing the plants home: Isolate any new purchases from your other houseplants for one to two weeks to make sure they are healthy and insect-free.

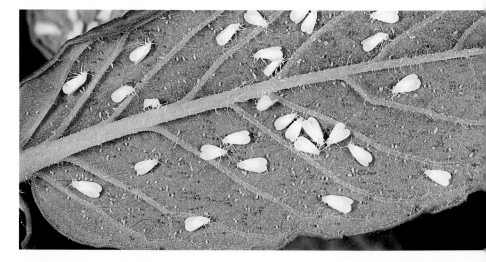

scale insects

top: Scale insects suck plant juices and live year-round indoors. They exude a honeydew that attracts sooty black mold (a fungus easily wiped off).

whiteflies

center: A nuisance outdoors, whiteflies become an annoying plague indoors. They usually arrive on plants you buy, so examine new purchases with an eagle eye.

aphids

right: These pale green, black, or reddish insects congregate on stems and buds of their favorite plants, sucking plant juices and leaving behind a sticky substance.

houseplant first aid

trouble sign	cause	remedies
Tiny, soft-bodied insects on growing tips, stems, buds, and undersides of leaves. Sticky substance (honeydew) on leaves.	Aphids	Hose plant with a forceful spray of water in the sink. Rinse larger plants in the shower. • Wash leaves and stems with soapy water (½ tsp. soap to 1 gal. water); rinse well in clear water. • Pinch off and discard affected parts.
Cottony masses where leaves join stems. Sticky substance (honeydew) on leaves.	Mealybugs	Dab bugs with cotton swabs saturated in rubbing (isopropyl) alcohol; rinse or wipe off the alcohol with warm water. Repeat every 7 to 10 days until you destroy all the insects. • Spray large plants with insecticidal soap. • Discard severely affected plants.
Rust-colored specks on leaves. Pale, dropping leaves. Tiny webs around leaves and leaf joints.	Spider mites	Mist plants frequently to prevent infestations that occur in hot, dry air. Mites are so tiny you often notice the webs first, after the problem has become acute. • Spray with soapy water. • Spray with insecticidal soap. • Discard severely affected plants.
Oval or round, stationary insects with shell-like covering on stems or undersides of leaves. Sticky substance (honeydew) on leaves.	Scale insects	Pinch off and discard affected parts. • Wipe off scale insects with a soapy rag. Use a toothbrush on stiff or strong stems of larger plants; rinse with clear water. • Dab with cotton swabs dipped in rubbing alcohol. • Spray young scales with horticultural oil (formulated for indoor use). Repeat treatments if necessary.
Dandrufflike insects congregating on undersides of leaves or rising in clouds around stirred plants.	Whiteflies	Vacuum off plants in early morning with a handheld vacuum. • Place yellow, sticky-coated cards near plants; discard as they fill. Repeat treatments to catch pests as they mature. • Wash hands after handling plants to keep from spreading eggs.
Wilting plant. Slimy, soft stem base, rhizome, or tuberous root. Often a foul smell when plant is pulled from pot.	Stem, crown, or root rot	Prevent by not overwatering and not allowing water to stand in pot saucer. Water less in winter, when plant is dormant. • Remove plant from container, cut off decayed area, replant in a pot with drainage holes, and don't water excessively—it may survive.
Seedlings flop over. Mushy spots at bases of seedlings.	Damping-off	Prevent by starting seeds in a sterile medium, such as a soilless germinating mix. • Do not overwater the medium. • You cannot save affected seedlings.
Stunted growth. Mottled, streaked, spotted, or curled foliage.	Viruses	Destroy plants—no cure exists—and dispose of them. Do not propagate; viruses transfer to new plants. • Wash hands and tools in soapy water after contact.
Flowers drop off prematurely.	Drafts or shock from moves	Keep plant away from cold drafts. • Don't move certain plants, such as holiday cactus, after flower buds form.
Buds shrivel and turn dry.	Uneven watering, low humidity	Water consistently (but don't overdo). • Raise humidity by misting foliage (not flowers), double-potting, or putting plant on a tray filled with pebbles and water.

from the pantry

Arm yourself with a few common household items in the fight against pests and diseases indoors. Ordinary liquid soap, water, cotton swabs, and rubbing alcohol go a long way toward curing many ills your plants may encounter. In the chart *at left*, the remedies progress from the gentlest to most extreme efforts.

Consistent care and attention help prevent many problems. When you check on your plant collections every day, be on the lookout for insects and diseases so you can catch them before they turn into incurable infestations.

Always use clean tools and hands when you work around your plants to avoid passing a problem from one plant to the next.

Be strong: Protect your other plants by discarding any plant that seems too far gone to help.

the
plants

common & botanical names

aeonium
Aeonium species and hybrids

african violet
Saintpaulia cultivars

agave
Agave species and hybrids

aloe
Aloe vera

aluminum plant
Pilea cadierei

amazon lily
Eucharis × grandiflora

angelwing begonia
Begonia coccinea

arrowhead plant
Syngonium podophyllum

asparagus fern
Asparagus densiflorus 'Sprengeri'

avocado
Persea americana

azalea
Rhododendron species and hybrids

bamboo
Phyllostachys species

banana
Musa species

barbados cherry
Malpighia glabra

bay tree (sweet bay)
Laurus nobilis

beefsteak plant
Iresine herbstii

bird of paradise
Strelitzia reginae

bleeding-heart vine (glorybower)
Clerodendrum thomsoniae

blue ginger
Dichorisandra thyrsiflora

blue trumpet vine
Thunbergia battiscombei

blue-flowered torch
Tillandsia cyanea

blushing philodendron
Philodendron erubescens

boston fern
Nephrolepis exaltata 'Bostoniensis'

bougainvillea (paper flower)
Bougainvillea glabra

brake fern (table fern)
Pteris species

burro's tail
Sedum morganianum

calla lily
Zantedeschia species and cultivars

cape primrose
Streptocarpus cultivars

cast-iron plant
Aspidistra elatior

cattleya
Cattleya species and cultivars

chenille plant
Acalypha hispida

chinese evergreen
Aglaonema modestum

chinese hibiscus
Hibiscus rosa-sinensis

cineraria
Cineraria hybrids (Senecio hybridus)

clivia (kaffir lily)
Clivia miniata

copperleaf
Acalypha wilkesiana

corn plant
Dracaena fragrans 'Massangeana'

crocus
Crocus hybrids

croton
Codiaeum variegatum

crown-of-thorns
Euphorbia milii

cyclamen
Cyclamen persicum

cymbidium
Cymbidium species and cultivars

dendrobium
Dendrobium species and cultivars

dumb cane
Dieffenbachia species

earth star
Cryptanthus species and cultivars

easter lily
Lilium longiflorum

egyptian star cluster
Pentas species and cultivars

elephant's-ear
Alocasia × amazonica

fiddle-leaf fig
Ficus lyrata

firecracker flower
Crossandra infundibuliformis

flamingo flower
Anthurium species and hybrids

flowering maple
Abutilon species and cultivars

gardenia (cape jasmine)
Gardenia jasminoides

gloxinia
Sinningia speciosa

golden candle (lollipop plant)
Pachystachys lutea

grape ivy
Cissus rhombifolia

heart-leaf philodendron
Philodendron scandens

hedgehog cactus
Echinocereus triglochidiatus

holiday cactus (christmas cactus)
Schlumbergera × buckleyi

ivy
Hedera species and cultivars

jade plant
Crassula ovata

japanese aralia
Fatsia japonica

jasmine
Jasminum species

jungle flame (flame-of-the-woods)
Ixora coccinea

kalanchoe
Kalanchoe species and cultivars

kentia palm (paradise palm)
Howea forsterana

lady's slipper orchid
Paphiopedilum species and cultivars

laelia
Laelia anceps

lantana
Lantana camara

lipstick plant
Aeschynanthus radicans

living stones
Lithops species

lucky plant (oxalis)
Oxalis species

madagascar dragon tree (rainbow plant)
Dracaena marginata

maidenhair fern
Adiantum pedatum

mandevilla vine
Mandevilla species and cultivars

moth orchid
Phalaenopsis species and cultivars

nerve plant (mosaic plant)
Fittonia verschaffeltii

never-never plant
Ctenanthe oppenheimiana 'Tricolor'

norfolk island pine
Araucaria heterophylla

oncidium
Oncidium species and cultivars

orange
Citrus sinensis

orchid cactus
Epiphyllum species and cultivars

ornamental pepper
Capsicum annuum

pansy orchid
Miltonia species and cultivars

paper-whites (paper-white narcissus)
Narcissus tazetta cultivars

peace lily
Spathiphyllum species and cultivars

Peperomia
Peperomia species and cultivars

persian shield
Strobilanthes dyeriana

persian violet (german violet)
Exacum affine

pincushion cactus
Mammillaria species

pitcher plant
Sarracenia species

plume flower
Justicia carnea

pocketbook plant
Calceolaria hybrids

poinsettia
Euphorbia pulcherrima and cultivars

polka-dot plant
Hypoestes phyllostachya

prayer plant
Maranta leuconeura

primrose
Primula species and cultivars

purple heart
Setcreasea pallida
(*Tradescantia pallida*) 'Purple Heart'

purple passion plant
Gynura aurantiaca

rabbit's foot fern
Davallia species

rain lily (zephyr lily)
Zephyranthes species

rex begonia
Begonia rex cultivars

rosemary
Rosmarinus officinalis

rubber tree
Ficus elastica

sanchezia
Sanchezia speciosa

scarlet star
Guzmania lingulata

schefflera (umbrella tree)
Brassaia actinophylla (*Schefflera actinophylla*)

shrimp plant
Justicia brandegeana

spider plant (airplane plant)
Chlorophytum comosum

staghorn fern
Platycerium species

strawberry begonia
Saxifraga stolonifera

string-of-beads plant
Senecio rowleyanus

ti tree (good-luck plant)
Cordyline terminalis

tree philodendron
Philodendron bipinnatifidum (*P. selloum*)

urn plant (silver vase plant)
Aechmea fasciata

variegated shell ginger
Alpinia zerumbet 'Variegata'

venus flytrap
Dionaia muscipula

wandering Jew
Tradescantia species and cultivars

wax plant
Hoya carnosa (*H. bella*)

zebra plant
Calathea zebrina

the plants

Abutilon species and cultivars
flowering maple

Light: High light year-round
Water: Allow soil to dry slightly between waterings; in winter, water more sparingly. Mist occasionally to deter spider mites.
Size: 3-4 feet tall
Produces yellow, orange, or salmon flowers from summer to fall. Fertilize every two weeks from spring to fall. Prune for size and shape in spring or fall. Propagate by stem cuttings.

Acalypha hispida
chenille plant

Light: Medium to low light
Water: Keep soil evenly moist year-round, slightly drier in winter. Mist leaves frequently to raise humidity and deter red spider mites.
Size: 3–6 feet tall
The tassel-like red or white flowers appear in summer and autumn. Fertilize every two weeks from spring to fall. Propagate by stem cuttings in spring.

Acalypha wilkesiana
copperleaf

Light: Bright or medium light
Water: Keep soil fairly dry year-round but mist the plant frequently.
Size: 4–6 feet tall
Produces colorful, mottled, and streaked leaves. Requires high humidity. Fertilize with every watering, using a diluted solution, from spring to fall. Propagate by tip or stem cuttings.

Adiantum pedatum
maidenhair fern

Light: Medium to low light
Water: Keep soil evenly moist year-round (slightly drier in winter); mist fronds frequently.
Size: 1-1½ feet tall; 2 feet wide
Beautiful hanging near a window or sitting on a pedestal. Appreciates the humidity of a bathroom. Fertilize monthly, except in winter. Propagate by division in early spring.

flowering maple

chenille plant

copperleaf

maidenhair fern

urn plant

aeonium

lipstick plant

agave

Aechmea fasciata
urn plant (silver vase plant)

Light: High or medium light
Water: Keep 1 inch of water in center well formed by leaves; occasionally empty water and let soil dry out.
Size: 18–20 inches tall
Feed by misting the leaves occasionally in spring and summer with diluted liquid fertilizer. As the flower fades, the plant dies but first produces offsets; propagate these and discard original.

Aeonium species and hybrids
aeonium

Light: High light year-round
Water: Keep soil fairly moist in spring and summer, water monthly in winter.
Size: 2–3 feet tall
A sculptural and excellent specimen plant. Fertilize every two weeks in spring and summer. Set in cool location (50 degrees) in winter. Propagate by leaf cuttings.

Aeschynanthus radicans
lipstick plant

Light: Medium light, or high light if you avoid direct sun at midday
Water: Keep soil evenly moist; water sparingly in winter. Mist leaves frequently.
Size: 2–3 feet long
Produces bright red flowers at the tips of trailing stems. Pot in loose soil mixture. Propagate by stem cuttings.

Agave species and hybrids
agave

Light: High to medium light
Water: In a shallow container allow soil to dry to a depth of 1 inch between waterings.
Size: 3–8 inches tall
Pretty in a dish garden of mixed succulents. Slow-growing and -spreading. Fertilize monthly in spring and summer. Propagate by offsets.

the plants

Aglaonema modestrum
chinese evergreen

Light: Medium to low light
Water: Allow soil to dry to a depth of 2 inches
between waterings. Mist frequently or grow on
a pebble-lined tray filled with water.
Size: 2 feet tall and wide
Tolerates less-than-perfect care. Keep plant
away from drafts. Fertilize every two weeks,
monthly in winter. Propagate by division or air
layering in spring or summer.

Alocasia × amazonica
elephant's-ear plant

Light: High light fall to spring; medium light
in summer
Water: Keep soil moist; in winter, let soil dry
out between waterings. Mist foliage frequently.
Size: 2½–4 feet tall
Not easy to grow. Fertilize every two weeks
with diluted fertilizer; do not feed in winter.
Propagate by division, suckers, or root
(rhizome) cuttings.

Aloe vera
aloe

Light: Medium light; appreciates some high
light in winter
Water: Water every week or two. Don't get
water on the leaves.
Size: 1–2 feet tall
Sap from a leaf soothes burns. Try growing
Aloe variegata, with striped leaves and late-
winter coral blooms. Fertilize monthly.
Propagate by suckers or new stem growth.

Alpinia zerumbet 'Variegata'
variegated shell ginger

Light: Medium to high light
Water: Allow soil to dry slightly between
waterings.
Size: 3–5 feet tall
A tolerant plant with gorgeous leaves and
porcelainlike flowers. Fertilize monthly.
Propagate by division.

chinese evergreen

elephant's-ear plant

aloe

variegated shell ginger

flamingo flower

norfolk island pine

asparagus fern

cast-iron plant

Anthurium species and hybrids
flamingo flower

Light: Medium light year-round
Water: Keep soil evenly moist, just slightly drier in winter. Mist leaves frequently.
Size: 9–12 inches tall
Scarlet-orange, white-spotted red, white, or pink flowers last up to two months. Blooms may need staking. Fertilize every two weeks in spring and summer. Divide in spring.

Araucaria heterophylla
norfolk island pine

Light: High to medium light
Water: Keep soil evenly moist. Mist once or twice a week.
Size: 3–6 feet tall
Long-lasting tree with appealing horizontal branches that turn from pale to darker green. Fertilize every two weeks in summer. Propagate by stem cuttings, but this method is recommended only for professionals.

Asparagus densiflorus 'Sprengeri'
asparagus fern

Light: Medium light
Water: Allow soil to dry out slightly between waterings (tuberous roots store water). Mist foliage occasionally.
Size: 2–3 feet tall
Not a true fern—modified stems form foliage. An excellent basket plant that's long-lived and easy to grow. Fertilize every two weeks from spring to fall. Propagate by division.

Aspidistra elatior
cast–iron plant

Light: Medium to low light
Water: Water when soil is dry to a depth of 2 or more inches.
Size: 2–2½ feet tall
So named because the plant survives neglect and less-than-ideal conditions. Occasionally wipe leaves with a damp cloth to remove dust. Fertilize every two weeks but don't worry if you forget. Propagate by division.

the plants

(Azalea) Rhododendron species and hybrids
azalea

Light: Medium light
Water: Keep soil evenly moist while plants
bloom; allow soil to dry slightly at other times.
Size: 1½–3 feet tall
For more than temporary color, keep plant
cool (50–60 degrees) and soil moist. Remove
faded flowers. Move plant outdoors in spring;
continue watering and fertilizing every two
weeks; bring indoors in late summer.

Begonia coccinea
angelwing begonia

Light: Medium light year-round
Water: Allow soil to dry to a depth of 1 inch
between waterings.
Size: 2½–3 feet tall
Coral or red pendent flowers. Fertilize every
two weeks while actively growing. Angelwing
begonias grow from fibrous roots. Propagate
by stem or leaf cuttings.

Begonia rex cultivars
rex begonia

Light: Medium light year-round
Water: Allow soil to dry to a depth of 1 inch
between waterings.
Size: 1 foot tall; 2–3 feet wide
Beautifully patterned leaves with silver, gold,
metallic red, purple, or pink splotches. Available
in scores of cultivars. Fertilize every two weeks
while actively growing. Propagate by stem or
leaf cuttings or division of rhizomes.

Bougainvillea glabra
bougainvillea (paper flower)

Light: High light; set outdoors in summer
Water: Keep soil evenly moist; water when
surface is dry. Water less in winter.
Size: 3–9 feet tall
Train on wire hoops; prune for bushiness.
Look for variegated types. Fertilize every two
weeks in spring and summer. Propagate by
stem tip cuttings (not easy).

azalea

angelwing begonia

rex begonia

bougainvillea

pocketbook plant

ornamental pepper

umbrella tree

zebra plant

Brassaia actinophylla (Schefflera actinophylla)
umbrella tree (schefflera)

Light: Medium light
Water: Let soil dry between waterings.
Size: 3–6 feet tall
A stalwart plant that forgives and survives your mistakes. Rinse leaves regularly. Fertilize every two weeks or monthly. Propagate by stem cuttings in spring.

Calathea zebrina
zebra plant

Light: Medium to low light
Water: Keep soil evenly moist, slightly drier in winter. Mist frequently.
Size: 1–2 feet tall
Spectacular markings on sleek foliage. May flower in warm, humid conditions. Cut off flower spike after it fades Fertilize every two weeks in spring and summer. Propagate by division.

Calceolaria hybrids
pocketbook plant

Light: Medium light
Water: Keep soil very moist at all times.
Size: 15–18 inches tall
Consider this a colorful but temporary indoor plant; purchase it in flower and discard afterward. Fertilize every two weeks during bloom. Propagate by seed (very difficult).

Capsicum annuum
ornamental pepper

Light: High light
Water: Keep soil evenly moist.
Size: 1 foot tall
The colorful stages of the fruit—green through yellow and orange to red—appear simultaneously on the plant. Keep plants out of children's reach, however, because the juice of the fruit causes burning if it gets near eyes or mouth. Discard plants when they finish fruiting. Propagate by seed.

indoor gardens | **111**

the plants

Chlorophytum comosum
spider plant (airplane plant)

Light: Medium light; needs bright light for best variegation, but direct sun scorches leaves
Water: Keep soil evenly moist. Mist foliage occasionally.
Size: 10–15 inches tall
A long-lived, easy-care plant that produces white flowers on cascading, long, wiry stems followed by plantlets. Excellent in a basket. Fertilize every two weeks except in winter. Propagate by division or rooted plantlets.

Cineraria hybrids *(Senecio hybridus)*
cineraria

Light: Medium light
Water: Keep soil barely moist–too much or too little water causes the plant to collapse.
Size: 1–1½ feet tall
Wonderful plants for color from midwinter to spring. Buy plants with many unopened buds. Keep them cool to prolong flowering; discard after blooming. Propagate by seed in summer.

Cissus rhombifolia
grape ivy

Light: Medium light year-round
Water: Allow soil to dry to a depth of 2 inches between waterings. Mist foliage frequently.
Size: 6–10 feet tall
Plant in a hanging basket or train around a window frame. Fertilize every two weeks except in winter. Propagate by stem cuttings. Kangaroo vine, *C. antarctica,* needs the same care.

Citrus sinensis
orange

Light: High light; put outdoors for summer
Water: Drench, then allow soil to dry to a depth of 2 inches or more between waterings.
Size: 10 feet or taller
Fun to grow indoors. Select a dwarf cultivar. Fertilize monthly in spring and summer. For fruit indoors, hand–pollinate the flowers using an artist's brush–you may get lucky!

spider plant

cineraria

grape ivy

orange

bleeding-heart vine

clivia

croton

ti tree

Clerodendrum thomsoniae
bleeding–heart vine (glorybower)

Light: Medium light
Water: Keep soil evenly moist but much drier in the winter. Mist frequently.
Size: 6–8 feet tall
Let this stunning plant trail from a hanging basket or train it up a trellis. Flowers are at the ends of stems. Feed with diluted fertilizer when watering. Propagate by stem cuttings.

Clivia miniata
clivia (kaffir lily)

Light: High light in spring; medium light the rest of the year
Water: Keep soil evenly moist in spring and summer; barely moist in fall and winter.
Size: 1½ feet tall
Striking plant with orange (or rare yellow) flowers. Fertilize every two weeks in spring and summer. Plant prefers to be potbound; delay moving it to a larger pot. Give plant a rest in winter (less water, some shade, and a 50-degree location) or it will not rebloom. Propagate by offsets with roots.

Codiaeum variegatum
croton

Light: Medium light; some sun in winter
Water: Keep soil evenly moist, slightly drier in winter. Mist often.
Size: 2–3 feet tall
A variety of color combinations and leaf shapes. Fertilize every two weeks in spring and summer. Propagate by stem cuttings.

Cordyline terminalis
ti tree (good–luck plant)

Light: Medium light
Water: Keep soil evenly moist; allow soil to dry to a depth of 2 inches in winter. Mist frequently.
Size: 3–4 feet tall
A long-lived plant with lance-shape leaves up to 2 feet long. Fertilize every two weeks except in winter. Propagate by stem cuttings.

the plants

Crassula ovata
jade plant

Light: Medium light; tolerates direct sun
in morning
Water: Allow soil to dry to a depth of 1 inch
between waterings. Water monthly in winter.
Size: 2–3 feet tall
Very forgiving, slow-growing plant. Fertilize
monthly from spring to late summer.
Propagate by stem or leaf cuttings (dry cuttings
for two days so ends form calluses).

Crocus hybrids
crocus

Light: Medium light
Water: Keep soil evenly moist.
Size: 3–4 inches tall
Forced into bloom indoors, crocuses add
lovely touches of color to windowsill gardens.
Fertilize monthly while blooms last. Plant
bulbs outdoors in the garden in spring or dry
the corms and plant in fall. Forced crocuses
will not rebloom indoors.

Crossandra infundibuliformis
firecracker flower

Light: Medium light, no direct sun
Water: Allow soil to almost dry out between
thorough waterings. Mist frequently.
Size: 12–15 inches tall
Not a long-lived plant. For success, provide
high humidity by grouping it with other plants
or setting it on a tray of wet pebbles. Fertilize
every two to three weeks in spring and
summer. Propagate by stem cuttings or seeds.

Cryptanthus species and cultivars
earth star

Light: High or medium light
Water: Allow soil to dry to a depth of 2 inches
between waterings; never let it dry completely.
Size: 2–5 inches tall, 6–8 inches wide
One of the easiest bromeliads to grow, with
beautifully colored foliage. Fertilize monthly by
misting the leaves with a water-soluble food.
Propagate by offsets.

jade plant

crocus

firecracker flower

earth star

never-never plant

cyclamen

rabbit's foot fern

blue ginger

Ctenanthe oppenheimiana 'Tricolor'
never-never plant

Light: Medium light; no direct sun
Water: Keep soil evenly moist in spring and summer. Allow soil to dry almost completely before watering in winter.
Size: 2–3 feet tall
Purple undersides of leaves add to the plant's beauty. Keep away from drafts. Needs high humidity; grow on a pebble-lined tray filled with water. Fertilize biweekly in spring and summer. Propagate by stem cuttings or offsets.

Cyclamen persicum
cyclamen

Light: Medium to low light
Water: Water when the soil surface is dry by standing the pot in water until saturated. Don't mist; grow on pebble-lined tray.
Size: 9–12 inches tall
A beauty with red, pink, white, or bicolor flowers. Requires a cool (55-degree) location to survive. Fertilize every two weeks while in bud and bloom. To keep plant beyond one season, dry tubers in late spring and repot in summer.

Davallia species
rabbit's foot fern

Light: Medium light; no direct sunlight
Water: Keep soil evenly moist. Mist regularly.
Size: 15–18 inches tall
Creeping rhizomes grow over the edge of the pot. Does not require the high humidity that most ferns need. Feed year-round with diluted fertilizer every three weeks. Propagate by rhizome cuttings.

Dichorisandra thyrsiflora
blue ginger

Light: Medium light
Water: Allow soil to dry to a depth of 2 inches between waterings, even more in winter.
Size: 2–4 feet tall
Fertilize every two weeks, spring to fall. Propagate by division or stem cuttings.
D. reginae has striped foliage flushed purple.

the plants

Dieffenbachia species
dumb cane

Light: Medium light
Water: Keep soil evenly moist, slightly drier in winter. Mist frequently.
Size: 2–6 feet tall
Keep out of reach of children and pets because the sap is toxic, swelling the tongue and throat. Fertilize when you water or every two weeks. Propagate by stem cuttings laid horizontally on potting medium (wash hands after handling).

Dionaia muscipula
venus flytrap

Light: Medium light; tolerates some direct sunlight
Water: Keep soil constantly moist (with rainwater if possible).
Size: 8–15 inches tall
Does best in a terrarium, where humidity remains high. Dry air wilts and kills it. Plant uses photosynthesis for food if insects, such as flies, are not available. Propagate by division.

Dracaena fragrans 'Massangeana'
corn plant

Light: Medium light; tolerates some high light
Water: Keep soil evenly moist. Water weekly; less frequently in winter. Mist often.
Size: 5 feet tall
An easy, slow-growing plant. Feed occasionally. Propagate by stem cuttings or air layering.

Dracaena marginata
madagascar dragon tree (rainbow plant)

Light: Medium light; some sun brings out the leaf color but avoid sun in summer
Water: Keep soil evenly moist. Water weekly; less frequently in winter. Mist occasionally.
Size: 2–6 feet tall
The easiest dracaena to grow. 'Tricolor' has cream-stripe leaves with red edging. Fertilize occasionally. Propagate by stem cuttings.

dumb cane

venus flytrap

corn plant

madagascar dragon tree

hedgehog cactus

orchid cactus

amazon lily

crown-of-thorns

Echinocereus triglochidiatus
hedgehog cactus

Light: High light year-round
Water: Keep soil barely moist; allow to dry almost completely between waterings.
Size: 3–10 inches tall
Slow growing. Branches and produces large blooms when it is a few years old. Fertilize monthly except in winter. Propagate by stem cuttings (let dry a few days before planting).

Epiphyllum species and cultivars
orchid cactus

Light: Medium light; no direct sun
Water: Keep soil evenly moist except during rest period. Mist frequently.
Size: 1½–2 feet tall
Mistakenly called night-blooming cereus. To promote the beautiful, fragrant flowers, summer the plant outdoors in a shady spot; bring indoors in late summer; rest it in midwinter by watering infrequently and setting it in a cool (50-degree) place. Fertilize twice a week in spring and summer. Propagate by stem segments.

Eucharis x *grandiflora*
amazon lily

Light: Medium light; no direct sun
Water: Keep soil evenly moist; water less for six weeks in early spring to promote flowering.
Size: 1½–2 feet tall
Pendulous, fragrant flowers. Stake or otherwise support the slender stems. Fertilize twice a week or monthly except in winter. Propagate by offsets.

Euphorbia milii
crown–of–thorns

Light: High light; tolerates medium light
Water: Water weekly; less often in winter.
Size: 2–3 feet tall
Easy plant if you don't overwater it. Look for yellow-flowering variety. Beware of the sharp spines. Fertilize monthly except in winter. Propagate by stem cuttings; be careful of the irritating sap exuded by the stems. Let cuttings dry for a day before planting them.

indoor gardens | **117**

the plants

Euphorbia pulcherrima and cultivars
poinsettia

Light: Medium light; tolerates some direct sun
Water: Keep soil evenly moist.
Size: 10 inches–3 feet tall
Fertilize every two weeks from fall to spring. Propagate by stem cuttings (let ends dry for a day). For more care tips, see pages 32–33.

Exacum affine
persian violet (german violet)

Light: Medium light
Water: Keep soil evenly moist.
Size: 6–8 inches tall
A biennial that most people treat as an annual and discard shortly after flowering ends in fall. Fertilize every two weeks. Can propagate by seeds but best to buy commercially grown plants.

Fatsia japonica
japanese aralia

Light: Medium light year-round
Water: Keep soil evenly moist.
Size: 3–6 feet tall (keep it small with pruning)
The bold, glossy green leaves make an architectural statement. One form features variegated leaves. Sponge leaves periodically to clean them. Plant prefers a cool location. Fertilize every two weeks in spring and summer. Propagate by side-shoot cuttings or air layering.

Ficus elastica
rubber tree

Light: Medium to high light
Water: Allow soil to dry almost completely between waterings.
Size: 3–10 feet tall
A workhorse that tolerates neglect and less-than-ideal conditions. Grows with a single stem unless you pinch the growing tip. Fertilize every two weeks or monthly. Propagate by stem cuttings or air layering.

poinsettia

persian violet

japanese aralia

rubber tree

fiddle-leaf fig

nerve plant

gardenia

scarlet star

Ficus lyrata
fiddle–leaf fig

Light: Medium light
Water: Water when soil surface feels dry.
Mist occasionally.
Size: 3–9 feet tall
Allow room to show off the large, glossy
leaves. Try growing the variegated cultivar.
Fertilize every two weeks or monthly.
Propagate by stem cuttings or air-layering.

Fittonia verschaffeltii
nerve plant (mosaic plant)

Light: Medium light
Water: Keep soil evenly moist but not soggy.
Mist frequently or grow in terrarium.
Size: 4–6 inches tall
An ideal terrarium plant, it prefers warmth and
humidity. Forms mounds of attractive foliage.
Fertilize monthly in summer. Propagate by
stem cuttings.

Gardenia jasminoides
gardenia (cape jasmine)

Light: Medium to high light; some direct sun
in winter
Water: Keep soil evenly moist, slightly less moist
in winter. Mist in summer but avoid blooms.
Size: 2–3 feet tall
Lush, fragrant white blooms and glossy deep
green leaves combine to make this a superb
plant. Set outdoors in summer if possible.
Fertilize biweekly from early spring to late
summer with an acidic, or azalea-type, food.
Propagate by stem cuttings in spring.

Guzmania lingulata
scarlet star (guzmania)

Light: Low to high light
Water: Keep central urn formed by leaves filled
with water. Keep potting medium evenly moist.
Size: 8–10 inches tall
The red flowers of this bromeliad are actually
bracts, which hide small white blooms. Fertilize
by misting the foliage occasionally with a
water-soluble food. Propagate by offsets.

indoor gardens | **119**

the plants

Gynura aurantiaca
purple passion plant

Light: High light
Water: Allow soil to dry to a depth of 2 inches between waterings.
Size: 3–4 feet long (trailing)
Purple hairs cover the green leaves and stems, giving the plant a velvety look and feel. Remove the orange, odoriferous flowers as they appear. Pinch plants to keep them compact and to promote new growth. Fertilize every two weeks in spring and summer. Propagate by stem cuttings.

Hedera species and cultivars
ivy

Light: High or medium light
Water: Allow soil to dry to a depth of 1 inch between waterings. Mist often to deter red spider mites.
Size: indeterminate (plant climbs as high or trails as long as you allow).
Look for variegated varieties, such as 'Glacier' and 'Gloire de Marengo,' as well as small-leaf types, such as 'Needlepoint.' Fertilize every two weeks. Propagate by stem cuttings.

Hibiscus rosa-sinensis
chinese hibiscus

Light: High or medium light
Water: Keep soil evenly moist, slightly drier in winter. Mist frequently.
Size: 3–4 feet tall
Long-lived. Prune to keep plant small. Fertilize every week or two in summer. Propagate by stem cuttings.

Howea forsterana
kentia palm (paradise palm)

Light: Medium to low light
Water: Keep soil evenly moist, slightly drier in winter. Mist frequently.
Size: 5–6 feet tall
Striking specimen plant. Fertilize every two weeks or monthly. Propagation impractical.

purple passion plant

ivy

chinese hibiscus

kentia palm

wax plant

polka-dot plant

beefsteak plant

jungle flame

Hoya carnosa (H. bella)

wax plant

Light: High to medium light
Water: Allow soil surface to dry slightly between waterings. Mist regularly only when plant is not in bloom.
Size: 1½–10 feet tall
Needs to be potbound and mature to bloom. New stems are bare; leaves appear later. Train on a wire form or trellis. Plant miniature *H. bella* in a hanging basket. Fertilize every two weeks from spring to fall. Propagate by stem cuttings.

Hypoestes phyllostachya

polka-dot plant

Light: Medium light; some sun in winter
Water: Allow soil to dry slightly between waterings.
Size: 10–12 inches tall
Pinch off growing tips to promote bushiness and flowers as they appear. Discard plant when it gets too leggy, usually annually. Fertilize every three weeks or monthly. Propagate by stem cuttings (several to a pot).

Iresine herbstii

beefsteak plant

Light: High to medium light; no direct sun in summer
Water: Keep soil evenly moist.
Size: 1½–2 feet tall
Beautiful foliage plant. Pinch growing tips to keep plant compact. Remove flowers as they appear. Fertilize every two weeks from spring to fall. Propagate by stem cuttings.

Ixora coccinea

jungle flame
(flame-of-the-woods)

Light: High light
Water: Keep soil evenly moist. Set pot on pebble-lined tray filled with water.
Size: 3–4 feet tall
Needs warmth and humidity to thrive. Best in a south-facing window. Fertilize every two weeks in summer. Propagate by stem cuttings.

indoor gardens | **121**

the plants

Jasminum species
jasmine

Light: High light
Water: Keep soil evenly moist, only slightly drier in winter. Mist foliage frequently.
Size: 5–10 feet tall
Train the lushly fragrant vining plant around a hoop or on a trellis. *J. humile* bears yellow flowers but lacks the heavy fragrance of Chinese jasmine, *J. polyanthum*, and common jasmine, *J. officinale*. Fertilize every two weeks when the plant is in bud and bloom. Propagate by stem cuttings.

Justicia brandegeana
shrimp plant

Light: High light
Water: Keep soil evenly moist, slightly drier in winter. Mist foliage occasionally.
Size: 2–3 feet tall
This easy-care plant produces colorful bracts (resembling shrimp) and white flowers. Fertilize monthly. Propagate by stem cuttings.

Justicia carnea
plume flower

Light: High to medium light
Water: Keep soil evenly moist, slightly drier in winter. Mist frequently.
Size: 3–4 feet tall
Dense spikes of flowers rise above large, highly veined foliage in summer. Cut plant back by half after blooming. Pinch the growing tips to keep the plant bushy. Fertilize every two weeks or monthly. Propagate by stem cuttings.

Kalanchoe species and cultivars
kalanchoe

Light: High light
Water: Allow soil to dry to a depth of 2 inches between waterings.
Size: 10–20 inches tall
Discard plant after flowering. Getting it to rebloom is difficult, but propagation is easy. Fertilize every three weeks while the plant blooms. Propagate by stem or leaf cuttings.

jasmine

shrimp plant

plume flower

kalanchoe

lantana

bay tree

easter lily

living stones

Lantana camara
lantana

Light: High to medium light
Water: Keep soil evenly moist; allow it to dry to a depth of 2 to 4 inches in winter.
Size: 12–14 inches tall
Many cultivars and colors. Fertilize every two weeks from spring to fall; don't feed in winter. Rest the plants in winter in a cool location; in late winter cut plants back to about 5 inches. Set plants outdoors in summer, if possible. Propagate by stem cuttings.

Laurus nobilis
bay tree (sweet bay)

Light: High to medium light
Water: Allow soil to dry to a depth of 3 to 5 inches (depending on pot size); in winter, water sparingly. Mist frequently.
Size: 3–4 feet tall (with pruning)
The source of culinary bay leaves. Provides plenty of fresh air; summer the plant outdoors if possible. Don't overwater in winter. Propagate by stem cuttings (not always successful).

Lilium longiflorum
easter lily

Light: Medium light; no direct sunlight
Water: Keep soil evenly moist.
Size: 2–3 feet tall
Buy this lily in bud and enjoy it as a temporary houseplant. Getting the plant to rebloom is unlikely unless you live in a warm climate and plant it in your garden. Stake stems to keep them upright, if necessary.

Lithops species
living stones

Light: High light
Water: Allow soil to dry almost completely between waterings. Don't water in winter.
Size: 1–2 inches tall
Curious plants that resemble stones until they burst into yellow bloom in late summer. Leaves shrivel after blooms fade; a new pair replaces the old. Don't bother to feed. Propagate by division.

the plants

Malpighia glabra
barbados cherry

Light: High or medium light; avoid direct midday sun in summer
Water: Keep soil evenly moist. Mist occasionally.
Size: 3–5 feet tall
Prune in late winter to control size and shape. Apply a diluted fertilizer every two weeks in spring and summer. Propagate by stem cuttings or seed.

Mammillaria species
pincushion cactus

Light: High light
Water: Allow soil to dry to a depth of 1 inch between waterings. In winter, let soil dry out before watering.
Size: 2–8 inches tall
Attractive plants for shallow pots. Some bloom when quite young. Water carefully around the edge of a pot so moisture doesn't get on the plants. Fertilize monthly except in winter. Propagate by offsets or seed.

Mandevilla species and cultivars
mandevilla vine

Light: Medium light; no direct sun
Water: Water when the surface of the soil dries. Mist often.
Size: 6–10 feet tall (prune after flowering for a smaller, bushier shape)
Often sold as *Dipladenia*. Train on a trellis or support the vining stems. Fertilize biweekly from spring to fall. Propagate by stem cuttings.

Maranta leuconeura
prayer plant

Light: Medium light
Water: Keep soil evenly moist. Mist often, preferably with rainwater.
Size: 8–10 inches tall
The decorative leaves fold up at night, unfurl in the morning. Needs high humidity and a warm location (70–75 degrees). Fertilize every two weeks except in winter. Propagate by division.

barbados cherry

pincushion cactus

mandevilla vine

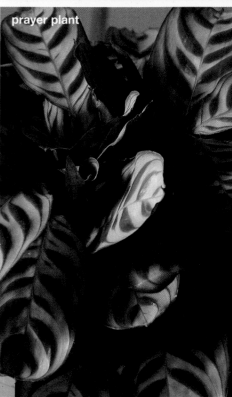
prayer plant

banana

paper-whites

boston fern

lucky plant

Musa species
banana

Light: High light
Water: Keep soil evenly moist at all times.
Size: 2–10 feet tall
Impressive plants that can produce fruit indoors. Buy a dwarf variety, such as 'Dwarf Brazilian' or 'Super Dwarf Cavendish.' Summer plant outdoors if possible; bring indoors in late summer. Fertilize every 10 days from spring to fall (bananas are heavy feeders). Propagate by offsets or division.

Narcissus tazetta cultivars
paper-whites
(paper-white narcissus)

Light: Medium light
Water: Keep soil barely moist.
Size: 15–18 inches tall
Enjoy the pure white blooms, then discard the plants. This particular narcissus needs no chilling period and blooms about six weeks after planting.

Nephrolepis exaltata 'Bostoniensis'
boston fern

Light: Medium light; tolerates some low light
Water: Keep soil evenly moist year-round. Mist frequently, especially in summer.
Size: 1 foot tall; 3–4 feet wide
Graceful plants for hanging in a basket or setting on a pedestal. Apply a diluted fertilizer every two weeks in summer. Propagate by plantlets or division.

Oxalis species
lucky plant (oxalis)

Light: High light
Water: Allow soil surface to dry between waterings to a depth of 1 inch in winter. Mist occasionally.
Size: 9–12 inches tall
In the family of the ubiquitous weed of outdoor gardens, lucky plant makes a charming houseplant. Fertilize monthly in summer. Propagate by division.

the plants

Pachystachys lutea
golden candle (lollipop plant)

Light: Medium to high light; no direct sun
Water: Keep soil moist from spring to fall;
slightly drier in winter. Mist occasionally.
Size: 2½–3 feet tall

Fleeting white flowers; yellow bracts last from
spring to fall. Maintain a bushy plant by
pinching off the growing tips occasionally.
Fertilize every two weeks except in winter.
Propagate by stem cuttings.

Pentas species and cultivars
egyptian star cluster

Light: High light
Water: Keep soil evenly moist.
Size: 18–20 inches tall (prune to keep neat)

Easy to grow, *Pentas* is a favorite of butterflies
outdoors. Prune plants in early spring and
repot them. Fertilize every two weeks or
monthly. Propagate by stem cuttings.

Peperomia species and cultivars
peperomia

Light: Medium light
Water: Water when soil dries to a depth of
2 inches. Water infrequently in winter.
Size: 8–10 inches tall

Easy to grow as long as you don't overwater.
Fertilize with diluted fertilizer monthly except
in winter. Propagate by stem or leaf cuttings.

Persea americana
avocado

Light: Medium light; no direct sun in summer
Water: Allow soil to dry to a depth of 1 inch
between waterings. Mist frequently.
Size: 3–8 feet tall

Fun to grow as a foliage plant but unlikely to
bear fruit indoors. Root the large seed from a
store-bought avocado in water, then pot in soil
with one-third of pit exposed. Pinch the stem
tip when it reaches 4-6 inches tall. Periodically
pinch growing tips to induce branching.
Fertilize monthly.

golden candle

egyptian star cluster

peperomia

avocado

tree philodendron

blushing philodendron

heart-leaf philodendron

bamboo

Philodendron bipinnatifidum (P. selloum)
tree philodendron

Light: Medium light; tolerates some shade
Water: Keep soil evenly moist, slightly drier in winter. Mist frequently.
Size: 3–4 feet tall
Forms a thick stem, or trunk, instead of climbing. Give it plenty of space because leaves spread to 3 to 4 feet. Propagate by cuttings from the base of the trunk or air layering.

Philodendron erubescens
blushing philodendron

Light: Medium light; no direct sun
Water: Keep soil evenly moist, slightly drier in winter. Mist occasionally.
Size: 5–6 feet tall
Guide stems and aerial roots onto a moss-covered pole or a cylinder of chicken wire filled with sphagnum moss that you keep wet. Fertilize every two weeks in spring and summer. Propagate by stem cuttings.

Philodendron scandens
heart–leaf philodendron

Light: Medium light; tolerates low light
Water: Keep the soil barely moist, drier in winter.
Size: 3–4 feet tall
Also known as sweetheart vine, it is easy to grow and has a tolerant nature. Fertilize every two weeks in spring and summer. Propagate by stem cuttings.

Phyllostachys species
bamboo

Light: Medium to high light
Water: Allow soil to dry to a depth of 2 inches between waterings; keep barely moist in winter.
Size: 4–20 feet tall
Most bamboos grow quickly and require large containers and high ceilings at maturity. Prune the top of the plant or just above a node to keep it in bounds. It may drop leaves at the onset of fall and winter. Fertilize every two weeks with a high-nitrogen fertilizer.

the plants

Pilea cadierei
aluminum plant

Light: Medium light
Water: Allow soil to dry to a depth of 1 inch
between waterings. Mist frequently.
Size: 8-12 inches tall
Very easy to grow. Prevent it from getting
straggly by frequently pinching the growing
tips. Fertilize every two weeks in summer.
Propagate by stem cuttings.

Platycerium species
staghorn fern

Light: Medium to high light, but not direct sun
in summer
Water: Allow medium to dry between
waterings. Water potted specimens from below.
Soak root ball of mounted plants in water for
five minutes, then drain.
Size: 1½-2 feet tall
Wrap root ball in sphagnum moss and tie it to
a piece of wood or bark with twine. Fertilize
monthly in summer with a water-soluble
fertilizer by spraying fronds or setting plant in
the water/fertilizer solution.

Primula species and cultivars
primrose

Light: Medium light; high light in winter
Water: Keep soil evenly moist, slightly drier
in summer.
Size: 8-15 inches tall
Delightful late-winter color. Summer outdoors
in a shady area; bring indoors in early fall.
Fertilize weekly while buds and blooms last.
Propagate by division or seeds.

Pteris species
brake fern (table fern)

Light: Medium light
Water: Keep soil evenly moist year-round.
Size: 8-24 inches tall
Grows well in a dish garden when young.
Look for variegated types. Fertilize weekly with
diluted fertilizer. Propagate by division.

aluminum plant

staghorn fern

primrose

brake fern

rosemary

african violet

sanchezia

pitcher plant

Rosmarinus officinalis
rosemary

Light: High light
Water: Keep soil moist year-round. Mist often.
Size: 2–3 feet tall
Common rosemary makes an excellent standard. Plant creeping-type rosemary in a hanging basket or as groundcover for an indoor tree or train it around a wire hoop. Summer the plant outdoors. Fertilize monthly. Propagate by stem cuttings or air layering.

Saintpaulia cultivars
african violet

Light: Medium light; filtered sunlight in winter promotes flowering
Water: Allow surface of soil to dry between waterings. Always water from below.
Size: 2–6 inches tall
The most popular of all flowering houseplants. Modern hybrids flower reliably given proper light and water. Fertilize every two weeks or use a diluted fertilizer with every watering. Propagate by stem or leaf cuttings or division.

Sanchezia speciosa
sanchezia

Light: Medium light; no direct summer sun
Water: Keep soil evenly moist, only slightly drier in winter. Mist frequently.
Size: 2–3 feet tall
A relative of the zebra plant, it requires high humidity. Produces tubular red flowers, but the large, glossy, ivory- or yellow-vein foliage is its most striking characteristic. Fertilize monthly. Propagate by stem cuttings.

Sarracenia species
pitcher plant

Light: Medium to high light
Water: Keep soil moist. Grow on a pebble-lined tray filled with water.
Size: 10–24 inches tall
This carnivorous plant prefers a cool location. Apply acidic fertilizer monthly. Propagate by division.

the plants

Saxifraga stolonifera
strawberry begonia

Light: Medium light; direct sun (but not from a
south window) helps leaf coloration
Water: Allow soil to dry to a depth of 2 inches
between waterings.
Size: 6–8 inches-tall; runners trail to 24 inches
Terrific hanging basket plant; easy to grow.
Look for the variegated form, 'Tricolor.' Fertilize
monthly in spring and summer. Propagate by
plantlets at end of runners.

Schlumbergera x buckleyi
holiday cactus (christmas cactus)

Light: Medium light
Water: Keep soil evenly moist except for about
Eight weeks after flowering. Mist frequently.
Size: 1–2 feet tall
Scores of hybrids and bloom colors. Encourage
blooms by summering plant outdoors in shade.
Don't move the plant once it sets buds. Fertilize
every two weeks except after flowering finishes.
Propagate by stem segment cuttings.

Sedum morganianum
burro's tail

Light: High light with some shade in summer
Water: Allow soil to dry to a depth of 1 inch
between waterings, deeper in winter.
Size: Trails 2–3 feet long
The fragile leaves tend to drop off if you
handle them too much. Fertilize occasionally;
plants in a soil-based mix seldom need feeding.
Propagate by stem cuttings.

Senecio rowleyanus
string–of–beads plant

Light: Medium to high light; avoid direct sun
in summer
Water: Allow soil to dry to a depth of 2 inches
between waterings; water just to keep soil from
drying out completely in winter.
Size: Trails 2–3 feet long
Tiny white flowers. Fertilize monthly except in
winter. Propagate by stem cuttings.

strawberry begonia

holiday cactus

burro's tail

string-of-beads plant

purple heart

gloxinia

peace lily

bird of paradise

Setcreasea pallida (Tradescantia pallida)
'Purple Heart'
purple heart

Light: High to medium light
Water: Allow surface of soil to dry out a little
between waterings.
Size: Trails 1½–2 feet long
Produces pink flowers in summer. Handle the
foliage with care. Fertilize every two weeks or
monthly except in winter. Propagate by stem cuttings.

Sinningia speciosa
gloxinia

Light: Medium light; no direct sun
Water: Allow soil surface to dry just slightly
between waterings.
Size: 8–10 inches tall
Hybrids bear large bicolor or spotted flowers.
To keep plants, overwinter the tubers in dry
soil; repot in fresh soil in spring. Fertilize every
two weeks in spring and summer. Propagate
by leaf cuttings or seed.

Spathiphyllum species and cultivars
peace lily

Light: Medium to low light (flowers best in
medium light)
Water: Allow soil to dry to a depth of 2 inches
between waterings. Mist foliage frequently,
especially in summer.
Size: 1½–2 feet tall
Tolerates low light better than most plants.
Produces long-lasting flowers. Fertilize every
two weeks in spring and summer. Propagate
by division.

Strelitzia reginae
bird of paradise

Light: High light
Water: Allow soil to dry to a depth of 1 inch
between waterings, deeper in winter.
Size: 2½–3 feet tall
Plants flower only if you set them where they
receive at least three hours of direct sun daily.
Fertilize every three weeks in spring and
summer. Propagate by division or seed.

the plants

Streptocarpus cultivars
cape primrose

Light: Medium light; no direct sun
Water: Allow surface of soil to dry
between waterings.
Size: 8–10 inches tall (miniatures also available)
Related to the African violet. Handle the
somewhat brittle leaves carefully. Fertilize every
two weeks or use a diluted fertilizer with every
watering; feed in winter only if the plant is in
bloom. Propagate by division or leaf cuttings.

Strobilanthes dyeriana
persian shield

Light: Medium light
Water: Allow surface of soil to dry between
waterings. Mist occasionally.
Size: 1½–2 feet tall
Leaves exude a silvery sheen. Pinch growing
tips to keep plant bushy. Fertilize every two
weeks. Propagate by stem cuttings.

Syngonium podophyllum
arrowhead plant

Light: Medium light; no direct sun in summer
Water: Keep soil evenly moist; in winter let soil
dry to a depth of half the pot.
Size: 3–4 feet tall
Fast-growing climber. Grow on a moss-
covered pole or plant in a hanging basket to
let stems trail instead of climb. Fertilize every
two weeks from spring to fall. Propagate by
stem cuttings.

Thunbergia battiscombei
blue trumpet vine

Light: Medium to high light
Water: Keep soil evenly moist.
Size: 5–6 feet tall
Another thunbergia, black-eyed Susan vine
(*T. alata*), also makes an excellent indoor plant
to grow up a trellis or trail from a hanging
basket. Fertilize every two weeks. Propagate by
seeds or stem cuttings.

cape primrose

persian shield

arrowhead plant

blue trumpet vine

blue-flowered torch

wandering jew

calla lily

rain lily

Tillandsia cyanea
blue-flowered torch

Light: High light
Water: Keep soil barely moist. Mist foliage occasionally.
Size: 8–10 inches tall
A bromeliad. Fertilize monthly with half-strength fertilizer. Propagate by offsets.

Tradescantia species and cultivars
wandering jew

Light: Medium to high light
Water: Keep soil evenly moist from spring to fall; in winter let soil dry to a depth of 2 inches.
Size: Trails 2 feet long
Fast-growing, easy-care trailing plants. Pinch growing tips to encourage bushiness. Fertilize every two weeks in spring and summer. Propagate by stem cuttings or division.

Zantedeschia species and cultivars
calla lily

Light: Medium light
Water: Keep soil very moist while plant is flowering, watering once a day if necessary; gradually reduce watering in late summer.
Size: 2–3 feet tall
Pot the rhizomes in spring. Summer plants outdoors if possible. *Z. aethiopica* produces white spathes on long stems. *Z. elliotiana* sports white-spotted leaves and yellow spathes. Look for dwarf cultivars. Fertilize every two weeks while plant is blooming. Propagate by division.

Zephyranthes species
rain lily (zephyr lily)

Light: High light
Water: Water thoroughly; allow soil to dry between waterings.
Size: 6–12 inches tall
Rain lily grows from a bulb potted up in late winter or spring for flowers in summer. Fertilize every two weeks while in bloom. Propagate by bulb offsets or seeds.

orchids

Epiphytic orchids adapt more easily to home conditions than terrestrial orchids. Orchids produce flowers that last from six weeks to as long as three months. Fertilize only when actively growing and flowering; use a diluted liquid fertilizer every week or a foliar feed every two to three waterings (spray it on). To provide humidity, mist leaves daily and place plants on a tray filled with moist pebbles.

Cattleya species and cultivars
cattleya

Light: Medium to high light
Water: Allow medium to dry to a depth of 1 inch between waterings.
Size: 10–20 inches tall
Easy. Plants usually do not require staking.

Cymbidium species and cultivars
cymbidium

Light: High light
Water: Keep medium evenly moist; never let the plant dry out.
Size: 10–30 inches tall
A terrestrial orchid that's difficult to grow in the home. It prefers cool (55-degree) temperatures in late summer to initiate flower spikes.

Dendrobium species and cultivars
dendrobium

Light: High light
Water: Keep soil evenly moist while in active growth. Allow to dry between waterings when growth is mature.
Size: 2–3 feet tall; some miniatures
Epiphytic. Let them rest briefly in winter.

Laelia anceps
laelia

Light: High light
Water: Allow medium to dry between waterings. Mist plant frequently.
Size: 6–24 inches tall
Epiphytic. Needs a dormant period. Mount on bark or pot in a mix of coarse bark and stone.

cattleya

cymbidium

dendrobium

laelia

pansy orchid

oncidium

lady's slipper orchid

moth orchid

The amount and frequency of watering an orchid needs depends on its growing medium as well as the temperature of the room and the intensity of light it receives. To determine whether the plant needs water, poke your finger into the medium. If the surface is dry but the interior is moist, check again in a day or two before watering. Generally, water orchids weekly; don't overwater them.

Miltonia species and cultivars
pansy orchid

Light: Medium light
Water: Keep the medium evenly moist.
Size: 10–14 inches tall
Velvety, rather small flowers with colorations that resemble a pansy. Grasslike foliage.

Oncidium species and cultivars
oncidium

Light: Medium to high light
Water: Allow medium to dry somewhat between waterings.
Size: 6–20 inches tall
Easy, tolerant plants. The tall, slender stems may require staking if you grow the plant in a pot rather than mount it on a slab of bark.

Paphiopedilum species and cultivars
lady's slipper orchid

Light: Medium light; no direct sun
Water: Keep medium evenly moist.
Size: 6–20 inches tall
The easiest terrestrial orchid to grow indoors. Produces exotic, long-lasting single flowers on long stems.

Phalaeonopsis species and cultivars
moth orchid

Light: Medium light, no direct sun
Water: Keep medium evenly moist, especially when they are young.
Size: 6–20 inches tall
Easy-to-grow orchid, with long-lasting flowers and thick, fleshy leaves. The main flowering season extends from late winter into spring.

sources

key

Catalog price subject to change

(B) bulbs

(E) equipment

(O) orchids

(P) plants

(R) roses

(S) seeds

Mail-Order Nurseries and Seed Suppliers

Brent & Becky's Bulbs (B) $1.00
7463 Heath Trail
Gloucester, VA 23061
877/661-2852
www.brentandbeckysbulbs.com

The Cook's Garden (S) free
P.O. Box 5010
Hodges, SC 29653-5010
800/457-9703
www.cooksgarden.com

Forestfarm (P) $4.00
990 Tetherow Rd.
Williams, OR 97544-9599
541/846-7269
www.forestfarm.com

Garden Pals, Inc. (E)
Mira Loma, CA 91752
800/666-4044
www.gardenpals.com

Gardener's Supply Co. (E) free
128 Intervale Rd.
Burlington, VT 05401
800/862-1700
www.gardeners.com

Glasshouse Works (P) free
P.O. Box 97
Stewart, OH 45778-0097
740/662-2142
www.glasshouseworks.com

Logee's Greenhouses (P) $4.95
141 North St.
Danielson, CT 06239-1939
888/330-8038
www.logees.com

Kartuz Greenhouses (P) $2.00
P.O. Box 790
Vista, CA 92085
760/941-3613

Nor'East Miniature Roses (R) free
P.O. Box 307
Rowley, MA 01969
978/948-7964
www.noreast-miniroses.com

Oak Hill Gardens (O)
P.O. Box 25
Dundee, IL 80118-0025
847/426-8500

Odom's Orchids, Inc. (O) $5.00
1611 S. Jenkins Rd.
Fort Pierce, FL 34947
561/467-1386
www.odoms.com

Park Seed (S) free
1 Parkton Ave.
Greenwood, SC 29647-0001
800/213-0076
www.parkseed.com

Peter Pauls Nursery (P) free
4665 Chapin Rd.
Canandaigua, NY 14424-8713
716/394-7397
www.peterpauls.com

Plant Delights Nursery (P) free
9241 Sauls Rd.
Raleigh, NC 27603
919/772-4794
www.plantdelights.com

Smith & Hawken (E) free
P.O. Box 431
Milwaukee, WI 53201-0431
800/940-1170
www.smithandhawken.com

Stokes Tropicals (P) $7.75
P.O. Box 9868
New Iberia, LA 70562
800/624-9706
www.stokestropicals.com

Worm's Way (E)
7850 N. Highway 37
Bloomington, IA 47404
800/274-9676
www.wormsway.com

index

index

index

photo credits

David Cavagnaro
67 (left) 71 (left) 108 (bottom center)
113 (bottom center) 115 (top center)
116 (top right) 117 (bottom center)
119 (bottom center) 125 (top left)
125 (bottom center) 129 (bottom
center) 130 (bottom center)
131 (top left) 133 (top left)
134 (top right) 135 (top left)

Ros Creasy
123 (top center) 128 (bottom center)

R. Todd Davis
98 (bottom) 115 (top center)
131 (top center)

Larry Hodgson–Horticom
126 (bottom center) 132 (top right)

Dency Kane
106 (top right) 111 (bottom center)
112 (bottom right) 113 (top center)
121 (top center) 123 (top left)
126 (top right) 128 (top center)
131 (bottom center)

Rosemary Kautzky
39 (top) 94 (top center) 95 (top right)
95 (top left) 97 (top center)
96 (top center) 99 (top right)
100 (top) 106 (bottom center)
108 (bottom right) 115 (bottom left)
115 (bottom center) 117 (bottom left)
120 (top center) 121 (bottom left)
121 (bottom center) 122 (top right)
122 (bottom center) 127 (bottom
center) 129 (bottom left)

131 (bottom left) 132 (bottom right)
133 (bottom center)

Oster & Assoc.
70 (top)

Jerry Pavia
107 (top center) 107 (bottom
center) 108 (top center) 108 (top
right) 111 (top center) 112 (top right)
114 (top center) 117 (top left) 117 (top
center) 119 (top left) 119 (top center)
122 (top center) 126 (top center)
128 (top right)

Ron West
100 (bottom) 100 (center)

metric conversions

U.S. Units to Metric Equivalents

to convert from	multiply by	to get
Inches	25.400	Millimetres
Inches	2.540	Centimetres
Feet	30.480	Centimetres
Feet	0.3048	Metres
Yards	0.9144	Metres
Square inches	6.4516	Square centimetres
Square feet	0.0929	Square metres
Square yards	0.8361	Square metres
Acres	0.4047	Hectares
Cubic inches	16.387	Cubic centimetres
Cubic feet	0.0283	Cubic metres
Cubic feet	28.316	Litres
Cubic yards	0.7646	Cubic metres
Cubic yards	764.550	Litres

Metric Units to U.S. Equivalents

to convert from	multiply by	to get
Millimetres	0.0394	Inches
Centimetres	0.3937	Inches
Centimetres	0.0328	Feet
Metres	3.2808	Feet
Metres	1.0936	Yards
Square centimetres	0.1550	Square inches
Square metres	10.764	Square feet
Square metres	1.1960	Square metres
Hectares	2.4711	Acres
Cubic centimetres	0.0610	Cubic inches
Cubic metres	35.315	Cubic feet
Litres	0.0353	Cubic feet
Cubic metres	1.308	Cubic yards
Litres	0.0013	Cubic yards

To convert from degrees Celsius to degrees Fahrenheit, multiply by $\frac{9}{5}$, then add 32.

To convert from degrees Fahrenheit (F) to degrees Celsius (C), first subtract 32, then multiply by $\frac{5}{9}$.